AT YOUR SERVICE

AT YOUR SERVICE

Tales from a railway dining-car

Michael Charman

·RAILWAY HERITAGE·
from
The NOSTALGIA Collection

This book is dedicated to the memory of Jack Attwood

'I have found some of the best reasons I ever had for remaining
at the bottom by looking at the men at the top.'

Frank Moore Colby, 1865-1925

ACKNOWLEDGEMENTS

I would like to thank the following people for their assistance in the preparation of this book: Terry Addicoat, Ted Beckerleg, Alun Joseph, Beryl Kimpton, Ray Kinghorn, Simon Plumb, Les Pender, David Staite, and the non-travelling staff at Penzance railway station.

A Silver Link book
from
The NOSTALGIA *Collection*

First published in November 1999

British Library Cataloguing in Publication Data

A catalogue record for this book is available from the British Library.

ISBN 1 85794 131 4

Silver Link Publishing Ltd
The Trundle
Ringstead Road
Great Addington
Kettering
Northants NN14 4BW

Tel/Fax: 01536 330588
email: sales@slinkp-p.demon.co.uk

Printed and bound in Great Britain

CONTENTS

INTRODUCTION

To have grown up in South West Cornwall during the 1940s and '50s was a magical experience. We had nothing of the material world, and all our pleasures were simple. During the summer school holidays we would spend every day on the beach. The days were long and it never seemed to rain. What fun it was to lie on your belly and look into a rock pool. The variety of living things within that small kingdom was wondrous to behold, and the truly amazing thing was that, with the changing of each tide, it would all be renewed. Time would be lost to a small boy and so enchanted would one become that the rest of the human race could be on another planet.

What greater pleasure could there be than to sit with your back against the outside of the swimming-pool, looking out over Mount's Bay? In Penzance the pool is built out into the sea, and was then and still is washed in white. The Battery Rocks that are attached to the pool were always my favourite hiding place. There I would be in a world of my own, where I would sit and look out to sea, feeling the slight spray on my face. Even on the hottest and driest days there was always a dampness in the air at that spot.

Then, when we were a little older, we would all put our best togs on, and on a Sunday evening we would promenade along The Promenade. In the 1950s lads liked to show off their teddy-boy suits.

Some went to great expense, with velvet lapels on their jackets, usually black. Fashion dictated that they should also sport a 'duck's arse', the supreme fashion pointer. The hair would be swept to the back of the head, where there was enough fullness for it to meet in the middle. If one could not afford Brylcreem then one would use sugary water to set it. The 'winkle-picker' shoes were so pointed that they were a job to get into. Never mind the pain – fashion was a hard task-master.

It was usual for the boys and the girls to walk up and down with their own gender. There was much looking and much whispering, and should a boy by chance decide to talk to one of the girls, he knew that when he left there would be much laughter of the hysterical type.

Since Penzance was such a small town you would see the same youngsters at the cinema, or at the Winter Gardens Ballroom, on any Saturday night. Saturday evening did not seem complete unless there was a fight outside the dance hall, and should you go into any pub late on a Sunday evening you would probably see the two participants drinking together, the previous night's combat completely forgotten. Not only that, but the chances that they were in some way blood-related were extremely high.

Every Good Friday the youth of Penzance, Newlyn and Mousehole would walk to Lamorna and back. I should think that 90 per cent of us were not suitably dressed, nor did we take enough food or drink for such a hike. Before the day was out there were bound to be blisters, followed shortly by tears. The boys would put on a brave front, and the girls would not miss it for the earth; after all, there might be a slight chance of a quick smooch with the boy of their dreams. If any of them had thought it out in the first place, I am sure that very few would have gone, but there were pressures on them to conform, just as there are today! At the end of the day I would say to myself 'never again', and at the time I was quite sincere about it, but come next year … off we would all go again.

One of the big events was the annual Corpus Christi fair, which was held on the fields in front of Lescudjack School. There was so much to do and to see. None of us had any money to speak of, but I remember that we all had a good time. I recall the excitement around the visiting boxing booth when the promoter boasted that if anyone could knock out one of his boys a £10 note would be his. There was a lad that the whole town knew of, who was usually one of the regulars that could be seen fighting outside of the Winter Gardens on a Saturday night. Up he would go to try to win that £10 note. There were plenty of claps and whistles from the crowd, and it was not long before the tent was bulging with Cornishmen ready to cheer on their man. Up jumps 'Jack the Lad', and there is much posing and posturing as the combatants parade around the ring. After what seems like an age the battle commences. They meet in the middle of the ring and shake hands, the bell goes … and so does our lad, with the first punch, on the floor accompanied by pool of blood. The shame of it. Even at that tender age I felt sorry for our boy. What would he do outside the dance hall on a

Saturday night! Surely no one would take him seriously any more.

On some fine days in the summer we could be seen up on Madron Carn. What a time we would have there! The scenery was very similar to that used in the cowboy films that were in vogue at the time. I always wanted to be Roy Rogers, and would imagine that a wooden stave placed between my legs was Trigger. 'Bang, bang! You're dead!' we would shout, and if your brothers or your friends failed to fall down you were very put out. That was not cricket … if you see what I mean. Just a few times I didn't mind being an Indian, if it was hot and sunny. No fool me! The thing that really did terrify me was when some fool would shout out 'Adders!' I was then, and still am, terrified of snakes. Madron Carn had the reputation of being the most infested place in Cornwall, yet in all the years I played there, I never saw one.

I do remember one day when I fell and cut my hand rather badly up there. Who should be there at the time but Sam Curnow, a well-known local character, who looked at the wound.

'Sorry, my ansom, but you best get down West Cornwall and let Sister McCarthy take a look.'

I almost fainted on the spot. Not from the wound but from Sam's suggestion that I should place myself in the hands of the dreaded Sister. It was obvious to me that he was right, and that I should go. Even to a child of my age I could see that it might need stitches. I thought that in some way I must pacify the turbulent Sister. It just so happens that to get to the West Cornwall Hospital from Madron, you have to go past Penzance cemetery, and by this time I was saying to myself, 'I'm sure that some flowers might be in order to ease the pain of her treatment.'

In my child's mind I was reasoning that it was not a bad thing to do to take a few flowers; after all, the people in the cemetery couldn't see or smell them, and if by my deed I should save myself some pain, then so be it. One consideration outweighed the other. As fortune had it I even found some brown paper to wrap them in.

What a sight I must have been with a tan that almost made me look like a refugee from Africa, and my hair bleached down to the colour of wheat in the sun. As a very nervous 12-year-old I went into the men's toilet, looked in the mirror and saw my dirty face. She would not like that, so I laid down my flowers and splashed water over my face. No comb, so I ran my fingers through my hair. I was so scared. My stomach was turning over, but it had to be done. I could have almost cried with joy when I discovered that Sister McCarthy was not on duty, and I am pleased to say that there was a very nice lady in her place. She looked at my hand, put the smallest of plasters on the wound, and reassured me that by the morning I could discard even that small dressing without coming to any harm. As for the flowers, she loved them, and she told me that her husband didn't give her flowers. She had been married for two years already, and her husband was very old – he was 28! After a kiss and a hug I went home.

Penzance in those days had three cinemas, the Ritz, the Savoy, and the Regal, of which the only survivor at the time of writing is the Savoy. In those days the manager of the Savoy used to be a Mr Lloyd, who only had one leg, poor man, and always had to walk with a stick. The reason I know this is that I used to court his daughter Marcia, and on more than one occasion I was entertained in his office. Once, in the middle of a conversation, he suddenly sprang to his foot and with his walking stick proceeded to hit the ceiling of his office, above

which was the projection room. When I asked him why he did this he assured me that he knew they were once again showing the wrong reel, and not therefore following the proper sequence. It was not unusual to be watching a cowboy film, then suddenly find that you were in the South China Sea. There would be the slow clapping of hands and stamping of feet, but it was all done in a good-humoured way.

One could always count on a complete show. There would always be a 'B' film followed by the news, trailers, advertisements, then the main feature. On a Friday the cinema would be packed, filling the place with enough cigarette smoke to set off any modern smoke alarm. Sometimes during the performance a man would walk up and down the aisle with a spray gun, tainting the atmosphere with a smell not unlike the dreadful aroma encountered in any hospital in those days.

Quite often there would be queues, and even when it was raining it did not seem to matter. The only problem with this situation was that there would be a smell that would linger through the whole performance. Even today, if I find myself jammed in a tube train on a wet day, my mind rushes back to the good old Savoy.

In those days you could get in for a shilling, but the most popular prices were the 'one and nines'. People were prepared to queue for hours to gain admittance at this price. A few were even prepared to pay 2s 9d. This was usually done by young men who were desperately in love. If they were seen entering the cinema hand in hand you knew that a wedding was on the way.

After the last show was over we would rush across the street to Mr Hawkins's fish and chip shop, and would walk home eating chips out of newspapers. Thirsty on arrival, we would hunt to see if there was any dandelion and burdock or Tizer hidden away; that would finish off the evening in grand style.

The Regal cinema was, at one time, a chapel, and if you sat upstairs you would find yourself facing the opposite balcony and would have to look either to the right or left, depending on which side you were sitting. The Regal was always known as 'the Flea Pit'.

The Ritz was in a different league altogether, and you could pay up to 4s 6d for a seat. It was here that I used to attend the ABC Minors, that is when I could afford the sixpence required for admittance. I learned one morning that the Ritz had 1,001 seats, the odd one being in the manager's office. It was here that I first saw Cinemascope. I was with my sister-in-law, and when the trailer came on we could not believe our eyes; there was a swish of the curtains, and there was *Seven Brides For Seven Brothers*.

One can hardly believe it now, but if it was an 'A' film, which meant that you could only be admitted with an adult, we would go up to a complete stranger and say, 'Can you take me in please, Mister?'

They usually did.

1

THE JOB

What to do when you left school. That was the question, especially if you had failed your eleven-plus. I suppose I could have worked on a farm. There was and still is plenty of agriculture in the West of Cornwall. If I had tried hard enough I could have gone to sea on the trawlers, or perhaps worked as a store-man at some establishment, but it was not to be. It was just as well that I didn't do any of these things, since when I was school-leaving age I was far from robust. In fact, an anorexic greyhound had more flesh on him than I had! I had always been thin right from being a young lad. When I look back now, I think what went wrong?

Prior to leaving school I had to go and see young Dr Dennis Leslie, who had his surgery in Morrab Road. I say young doctor because I remember his father, who was Dr William Leslie. Even then Dr William must have been getting on apace. I remember that he always had a dressing on one of his hands. There had been a terrible accident experimenting in the early days of X-rays, and he had been badly injured.

Young Dr Dennis asked me when I was to leave school, and when I told him he asked if I had any idea of what I wanted to do. I said that I had no idea. He stared at me for a long time, cigarette in mouth. A great deal of ash had fallen on to his waistcoat but it did not seem to bother him. He then put out the cigarette, pulled

a face, and tilted his chair slightly on to its two back legs. Still nothing was said. Now he was pulling down his top lip with his teeth, and was gnawing at his moustache.

At last he said, 'I have the very thing for you – you ought to join the Forestry Commission. All those trees, all that fresh air would do you the world of good and get some meat on those bones of yours.'

I was quite taken aback by this statement. Not in my wildest dreams had I thought of anything like that. To work perhaps in Woolworths, or Simpsons, the men's outfitters, somewhere where it was warm and civilised – not out in all the elements. No! That would not do at all. The man must be having a brainstorm, I thought.

Like a good many folk in Penzance, I was to get to know young Dr Dennis well over the years. I remember that it was about this time that I had to visit him with a nasty rash. In those days you just let yourself into the front room of his house, and when he was ready you took turns to go in. That evening I was sitting there with about nine others, and when he was ready he popped his head around the door, looked at us all, then, pointing to one man, said, 'You get in the other room and roll your sleeve up, you and you go home. Now! Who's the first in the line of dodgers?'

I don't think he was in a very good mood that day!

Much later, on one of my many trips

back to Cornwall, I was having a drink in the Swordfish in Newlyn with a group of trawlermen when young Dr Dennis's name came up in the conversion. I was informed that he was the port doctor, and had been for some time. One trawlerman told me a story about himself and Dr Dennis. It seems that this man was out at sea with the others of the crew, not far off Land's End, when the skipper died while slumped over the wheel. As you might expect, the men were most upset at this. Eventually they got through to Dr Dennis on the short-wave radio.

'Whatever you do, lads, you must not move him. Do you hear me? This is essential. Make for Newlyn and I will be there to meet you.'

One of the crew replied, 'How the hell can we steer with him slumped over the wheel?'

'I don't care what you do, but the man must not be moved. How you sort it out is up to you. Do you hear me?'

Off they set to return to Newlyn. As they came past Mousehole they had to turn left to get into Newlyn harbour, so they took the skipper down and laid him on the deck. When they had a clear run in, they picked him up again and slumped him over the wheel. Sure enough, Dr Dennis was waiting, and as he was boarding the trawler he said, 'Cleverest bloody corpse I've ever seen!'

It is some measure of the man that on occasions when I have been home in Penzance I have booked to visit him as a patient, just to have a word with him. When my brother rang and told me of his passing, I was filled with sadness. He was quite a character.

Anyway, after his comments about the Forestry Commission it was with some trepidation that I set off for the Labour Exchange. On the way I saw 'Willie Rubber Neck' in the Green Market. What a life us kids gave that poor man, but he never seemed to mind. Bless him. He was one of God's special children.

I know that as I was walking down the road I was thinking to myself that I had not lived very long, and here I was going out to try and look for a job. It didn't seem right somehow, with my childhood already gone. What did frighten me was the idea that nobody would want me to work for them. After all, I had nothing to offer. I could count to a degree, but my spelling was absolutely atrocious. In one school report the geography teacher wrote, 'The lad does well to find his way home!'

I had never done anything outstanding at school. In the exams I was always about halfway down in most subjects. The only time I was top of the class was the year that I sung 'Bless This House', but it was never to be repeated. I was not too hot at sport either, so you may say that I was a non-starter in most things. So, as you can imagine I was not looking forward to seeing the man at the Labour Exchange.

'Not a lot to offer, have you lad? Have you always been as thin as that?'

After answering the affirmative, I sat there with my shoulders hunched while the man went through the index. He was talking to himself, saying things like 'I don't think so…', pushing each card back into its rightful place in the index. I seemed to have been sitting there for some considerable time. I hope I don't land up with a job like yours, I thought, but I kept that to myself.

A girl of about 17 came into the room and put a file in front of the man. She looked at me in a very strange way, then leaned over the desk and, coming quite close to me, breathed heavily and said, 'Hi, my ansom. Who do you belong to?'

I was quite taken aback by this forward behaviour of hers. The man said, 'Now Sue, that will be enough, thank you. We don't wish to embarrass the young man.'

Too late by far. The young man was already embarrassed. As she got to the door, she turned and, shaking her long blond hair, blew me a kiss. As the man's desk was in the middle of the room, together with several others, he did not see this action, but I could feel myself blushing. Who did she think she was – Veronica Lake?

'Pigs,' the man said.

I said nothing.

'Pigs.' He said it again.

'Pigs?' I replied.

'Yes,' he said. 'Pig farm out Drift way. One pound eighteen and sixpence a week. Have you got a bike?'

'No,' I replied. I had no intention of getting one either.

'Pity that – could have been a good job at the end of it.'

He must be short of oxygen, I thought. Given the choice I would rather have gone to the trees than to the pigs. He started sucking his teeth, and was making the most weird noise. Thinking about his dinner, I thought.

'Stable Hobba,' he said.

I said nothing.

'Stable Hobba.' He said it again, and looked at me hard. 'Did you hear what I said?'

I told him that I had.

'Good – it seems that they have a vacancy for a general hand at the fertiliser factory.'

I knew about fertiliser as my girlfriend, Marcia Lloyd, worked in a shop that sold fertiliser opposite Lloyds Bank, at the top of Market Jew Street. However, he could tell by the look on my face that this was another non-starter. Yet again he consulted the index, then he said the golden words: 'Dining cars'.

Yes, they wanted a pantry boy on the 'Cornish Riviera Express'.

'As far as I can see the main job is to do the washing up, but there are many other things to do as well. Go to London one day and back the next. Uniform provided plus all meals. What do you think?'

What did I think! Well, I thought even I can do some washing up. Food! Real food! This was all too much to take in at once. He gave me a chitty and told me to report to the chef on the 'Riviera' the next day. The train should be at the platform if I got there for 8.30.

For the rest of the day I was in a dream. What an adventure it would be, and I would have a uniform to wear as well. However, if I'd known then what the uniform was like, I wouldn't have been so keen.

I only had one pair of shoes and there was a hole in the bottom of the right one. I put some newspaper into it; as long as it did not rain, all would be well. My shirt had a frayed collar. I only had two pairs of trousers, a dark brown pair and a mid-grey pair. The first were starting to show through the knee, and the grey ones were not too bad but perhaps a little short. Until last week I had a belt as well, but unfortunately that had broken as I was climbing a tree in Penlee Park, so I was making do with an old neck-tie. I did have a jumper; it had red and grey vertical stripes across it. At least it would go with the trousers, and it only had one small hole in the side, so with luck no one would see it. My jacket was a mucky beige and it had leather patches on the elbows. I was quite proud of these – they were quite the in thing. Dr Dennis had them on his jacket as well, so they must be. It could have done with being a little shorter in the arm, but you cannot have everything. It was no better or worse than those of any of the other children in our street. With so many of us at home things were passed down and we were grateful for them, and as I was the next from the youngest, they were well worn by the time they reached me. My

Dressed up and ready to enter a man's world!
Author

stepmother, May, did all she could for us. Even my brothers, Ivor and Garry, were not hers, but we were treated as if we were.

I was just getting over a boil on my neck, which had been painted with some yellow stuff at school by the nurse. It was on its last legs, but I thought it might be a good idea, when I went for the interview on the train the next day, to lean my head at a tilt. With luck they would not notice it, but I quickly came to the conclusion that perhaps this might not be the right thing to do. They might think I had a permanent disfigurement.

When I got home to Alvern Buildings and gave my stepmother the news about the job, she was pleased. I think that from her point of view it meant one less mouth to feed, and because of that slightly less

worry. I don't know where she got it from, but a sixpence appeared, and I was dispatched for a sixpenny haircut at a shop opposite St John's Hall. I washed my hair with carbolic soap – I had to be spick and span for the morning. My stepmother gave me another tuppence, and off I went down to Mr & Mrs Burton's little shop in Stanford Terrace to get a pair of shoelaces. This indeed was my lucky day. I was often sent to the little shop, and the items that I remember buying the most were gas mantles. To me they were always a wonder – like a cobweb, but man-made, and should you touch them with your finger they would fall to dust.

The next morning I set off down past the Police Station, past St John's Hall, through the Green Market; down the long slope through Market Jew Street; over the road and into the station. I had been to the station quite a few times to look at the trains. Many times I had walked out to Long Rock, which is not far from the station and where there is a gap allowing access to the beach. Quite often you would find there some coal that had fallen off a train, and if you returned home carrying some you were very popular indeed.

Just past the platforms on the way out of town is a place called Chyandour. Here there are three tunnels that pass under the railway and come out on rocks on the other side. It was to this place that I escaped when I decided to run away from home following a row with my stepbrother John. I grabbed a raw turnip, a small fishing net, and some matches. I thought I could catch some fish in the rock pools and cook them over an open fire. I must have stayed under the tunnels for at least half an hour before deciding that perhaps the feather bed, which I shared with John, was a sight more comfortable than sitting with my back to the rocks. It was at least a quarter of an

Penzance station, with its refreshment room, Guinness advert and vintage cars, just as I remember it in 1952. *Lens of Sutton*

hour after returning home that I started talking to John again. That should show him…

The train stood at number 1 platform. The first man to greet me was the chef, Sid Reed. Many years later, after he was made redundant by British Rail, he was to take up new employment as a chimney sweep, but on that day he looked very grand in his kitchen whites with his tall hat on and a spotless white apron around his waist. I never saw Sid in the kitchen without his hat on – never. He was a very busy man – always on the go, but a very accomplished cook.

Sid took me through to the Third Class Saloon. At the first table were two of the other staff, one a kitchen porter, Clem Bowden, and the other an attendant. They were eating toast and it looked very inviting to me. Sid told me to sit down at the table with them and gave me a glass of tea. It must have been the way I was looking at the toast, because it was not

long before the attendant, who I was later to learn was called Dickie Mitchell, asked me if I would like some. Indeed I would, and I woofed it down like the runt of an unwanted litter, only to be offered another slice. It was then that I decided for certain that this most definitely was the job for me!

Sid then took me to the pantry and told me about the job, and needless to say it all went in one ear and out of the other. I met all the staff and it was getting most confusing. There seemed to be so many of them, and there did not seem to be much room to move about in.

After this I met the conductor, Cyril Turner. He was a short man, with a strange manner about him. His son worked on the cars as well, but not with us.

'Pleased to meet you, sir,' I said.

'No need to call me sir, son. What school did you go to?'

I told him that it was Lescudjack. He asked me the name of the headmaster, and

I replied that it was Mr Hitchings. He asked me about home, and I gave him all the information he wanted. He then said something very strange.

'How do you spell "machine"?'

Needless to say I could not.

'I thought not!'

He seemed to smile as if I had passed some sort of test. Strange man, I thought, and I was right!

He then said, 'Have you got a toilet bag?'

What on earth is he on about, I thought. What is a toilet bag? I had a vision in front of me of doing your toilet into a bag, but surely not – it must mean something else.

'Do you have any pyjamas?'

He was asking now – what next? No I did not have any. I had seen them in the window at Simpsons and that was as near as I had been to them up to now.

'Pantry boys don't stop long. Too much hard work for them. Don't know what we're turning out from school now. The country's going to the dogs.'

I said nothing and looked at my feet – only to see that I had odd socks on. I moved about and hoped that he would not see them.

'Yes,' he was saying. 'Start the day after tomorrow.'

That was it – I was in. Dickie Mitch, as I was to call him, looked at me and winked, and I burst into a smile. I had done it!

'That's it, my ansom, bloody hard work, but it's a job.'

I smiled back. 'Hard work don't worry me any.'

He tapped the top on my head, as you might a friendly dog. 'Look, my lover, try not to wear odd socks.'

I blushed and looked at the floor.

Later I walked up town as if on a cloud. I had done it! Not bad for a dimwit like me, I thought.

2
THE 'RIVIERA'

The first day I started work back in 1952 the train was not at Penzance station, so I had to walk out to Slopers at Ponsandane, just past Chyandour on the way out of town. Now that I was employed by British Railways I was able to walk along by the track, although I was very nervous and made sure I kept clear of the rails. When I reached the train I looked up. I could not believe how tall it was.

There was no way I could climb up on my own, so I shouted as hard as I could. I saw a man's head pop out of the window. It was Ernie Keneally, the relief chef. He looked down on me.

'What do you want, son?'

I looked up and said, 'I'm the new pantry boy. Can you help me up please?'

Ernie opened the door, went down on one knee and put his hand down, and

The Severn Valley Railway's preserved Great Western Railway restaurant car, like those still running on the Western Region in the early years following nationalisation. This view shows how high the carriage is to enter from ground level, especially for a young boy! *David Harvey*

soon I was up and in the dining car. Ernie was an Irishman and was plain-talking at the best of times.

'What shall I do, chef?' I asked.

He thought for a moment, then said, 'If you have any sense you'll go back home.'

To be honest he did not say that at all. What he did say decency forbids me from putting into words. I was soon to learn that Ernie was somewhat excitable, and a devoted father to his teenage daughter. Later he became a widower, remarried and emigrated to Australia to become a chef on their restaurant cars.

Next I met the kitchen porter and the kitchen boy, and not long after that the saloon staff started to arrive, then we went very slowly back into the station and the conductor boarded. It was not the same man I had seen at the interview, but was Freddie Greville, the relief conductor. To me he looked like Franz Hals's painting of 'The Laughing Cavalier'.

He gave me a uniform to try on. The material was a rough serge. There was a jacket with many brass buttons on the front done up to the neck, and the collar was to chaff me unmercifully. The trousers were of the same material, and to finish off there was a pill-box hat complete with a black tassel and a leather strap, which was very tight, to be worn under the chin. The sleeves of the jacket were too short. I got changed in the toilet and, when I turned around and looked into the mirror, I could have cried. I looked so stupid. When the rest of the crew saw me they fell about laughing. They wore the old Great Western Railway colours – brown trousers with a thin black stripe down the seam of the leg, cream waistcoats with gold buttons, and cream 'monkey jackets' with one gold button and chocolate-brown lapels. Their shoes were dark brown, their shirts were white with a detachable collar, and a chocolate-coloured tie to match the lapels completed the outfit.

The 'Cornish Riviera' left Penzance at 10.00am and arrived at Paddington at 4.40pm. It was known to railwaymen as the 'Limited', indicating that there were a limited number of seats available on the train. During the week it would comprise ten coaches, but on a Saturday there would be 15. It was absolutely imperative that the coaches should be in the 'chocolate and cream' of the old GWR. On the down trip we left Paddington at 10.30am and arrived at Penzance at 4.55pm. If it was late into Penzance, Mr Lyons, the station master, would want to know why. He was a small man with a moustache, always smart and held in a great deal of respect by his staff.

On Saturdays in the summer the 'Riviera' was run in up to five parts, with trains running from St Ives, Penzance, Falmouth and Newquay. I can remember going direct from Truro to Paddington on one of those days. There was a special lunch menu of cold ham salad, roll and butter, and the sweet was tinned mixed fruit, which cost 4s 6d. We did literally hundreds of these meals, but did not mind as they were 'plate service' where the usual meals were 'silver service'. I would rush up and down the coaches selling Kia Ora squash at sixpence a time. We also served coffee and biscuits down the corridor, as well as in the dining car.

One of the jobs expected of the pantry boy was to use the wooden butter pats to make little balls of butter. The knack to this was to make sure that the butter was neither too warm nor too cold. There was quite an art to it. He was also expected to cut the grapefruit in half and into segments. Another of his jobs was to arrange the flowers,which would come on fresh each day at Paddington and Penzance. The Cornish ones were usually either anemones or violets, depending on the season. The 'Royal Duchy', another named express train on which I was to

A damaged but precious photograph of the London 'Limited' crew, showing the style of uniforms worn. I am second from left, with Les Pender second from right. *Author*

The 'Cornish Riviera' in full flight behind ex-GWR 'King' Class 4-6-0 No 6008 *King James II*. *Lens of Sutton*

work, also had fresh flowers, and if I remember correctly so did the specials to Newbury Races.

The actual layout of the pantry was fascinating – there were so many nooks and crannies. There was a small bar for the dispensing of drinks. If you stood in front of the sink and looked up, there was a row of wooden strips into which you would slide cups rather like the racks used in some pubs today. Behind you there were places into which to slide tea plates. The whole pantry was very compact, and the design was terrific, and would put any latter-day designer to shame. In the corridor there was a wedge-shaped cupboard packed with shelves; this was for the storage of butter and fruit juice. Fresh ice was obtained at Penzance and Paddington.

At Penzance, the kitchen boy and pantry boy would get a large railway trolley, put all the previous day's swill and rubbish on it, and pull it around to the back of the station where there was a place to dump it. At Paddington there were special porters to do this for you. Also at Paddington we would take on board both wet goods, fish and meat. Because of the timings of the train it was imperative that all this activity should go like clockwork, and it did.

The 'Cornish Riviera' started its life in 1904 leaving Paddington at 10.10am. It went via Bristol to Plymouth, a total mileage of 245.6, and at its inception was the longest non-stop run in the world, travelling at an average speed of 55.2mph. In Cornwall it stopped only at Truro, Gwinear Road and St Erth. Initially it had six coaches, which went all the way to Penzance. By 1906 the train was going via Westbury and left Paddington at the traditional time of 10.30am. It had 'slips' (separately controlled carriages detached from the rear without the main train stopping) for Westbury and Exeter, and the next year there was an extra slip for

The author having a nostalgic look at the kitchen in the Severn Valley Railway's preserved GWR restaurant car. Beyond, in the pantry, is David Staite, who used to work on the 'Cheltenham Spa Express' when I worked on the 'Limited'. On the 'Limited' in the 1950s the panelling was wood, but more recently has been clad in stainless steel for hygiene reasons. *Author*

Inside the pantry, with all its 'nooks and crannies'. *Author*

Taunton. Each slip had a guard, and if you were travelling in a slip there was no way you could walk through to the dining car. I imagine it must have been quite a job making sure that no late passengers alighted from the wrong carriage.

In 1917, during the Great War, the 'Limited' departed from Paddington at 10.15am, with no restaurant car. It had many stops, including Westbury, Taunton, Exeter and Newton Abbot, and all principal stations to Penzance. From July 1919 it reverted to the 10.30am departure, non-stop to Plymouth in 4½ hours with slips for Taunton and Exeter, and from the October timetable of that year an extra slip was added for Westbury. It is interesting to note that in 1904 the dining capacity for First Class was 18 and Third Class 32, while in 1929 it was 24 First Class and 95 Third Class.

When I looked out of the window on that first day I was excited to see so many things for the first time. What a sight I had at Saltash on the Tamar – all those Royal Navy ships and the Royal Albert Bridge. It it was all too much to take in.

The best part of our day was when we had our own lunch. We could not take too long for this because we had to get on with the teas. My first lunch was curry – I thought it would burn a hole in my throat and with my eyes running I ran to the pantry to get a glass of water. When I returned to the table I noticed that the others, except Ernie, were having cold meat and salad. Ernie was a bit heavy-handed with the curry powder, but it gave me a taste for curry that has not left me.

How I made it through the first day I have no idea. All that washing up! I thought it would never end. The kitchen staff would wash the large lunch plates, and also the silver plate vegetable dishes, but that was about all. The rest came to me. Now I look back and I wonder how I managed it, but I did.

I was informed by Freddie Greville not to mix with lads from other trains when we arrived at Paddington; after all, being a 'Limited' boy I was a cut above the rest. For a small fee I used to clean his shoes and the brass buttons on his uniform, the latter being done at the digs in London. In those days we used to send off our shirt collars by post in a little box, which held five and had little brass corners on it. They would be cleaned and starched and returned to us for a fee of 1s 6d. Later we bought plastic ones from Woolworths, but they were not very good, making you feel hot and uncomfortable. Later, when I was made up to attendant, I used to walk up and down the restaurant car in the sidings at Old Oak Common in London and admire my reflection in the windows – I felt I looked rather like Peter O'Toole in *Lawrence of Arabia*…

On my second day I made my first 'down' trip on the 'Cornish Riviera' from Paddington to Penzance, still with the Cornish crew. We had been busy and I felt quite exhausted. By the time we got as far as Camborne I had had more than enough of washing up – I was dead on my feet and my hands were in a shocking condition. The pantry had a wooden sink and to help get the grease off the plates we used raw soda. We also had a round tin, like a baked bean tin, with one end removed and the other with holes punched into it. A bar of soap was placed inside the tin and shaken around in the hot water to try to create a lather.

We did not stop at Camborne, but as we passed by one of the staff suddenly shouted, 'Now!'

All hell was let loose. I was grabbed by the kitchen porter and one of the attendants and in no time at all I was completely naked. They dragged me screaming into the vestibule space between the kitchen and the pantry, and the door was firmly shut. Once they had

A restaurant car conductor's report made out by Freddie Greville in 1948, highlighting one of the hazards of working aboard a moving train. '...While crossing over on to the LMS line at Standish Junction [between Gloucester and Stroud] asst cook Rodden was thrown off balance while removing a pot from the stove. On trying to recover his balance he was thrown against the window, which broke with the impact, and cut Rodden's wrist and fingers. He attended Penzance Hospital and the doctor's report is attached...' *Author's collection*

me on the floor they proceeded to stamp me all over, and I mean all over, with the rubber stamp used when ordering the stores; it had 'Limited Two' embossed on it. When this was complete they got a linen bag – these were huge, as we used to put at least 20 dirty tablecloths into them and send them to the laundry to be washed – and enveloped me in it. After this all sorts of things were tipped on top of me: potato peelings, grapefruit skins, used tea-leaves, ice-cream, gravy, old cabbage, fish heads – and so it went on. My head was pushed inside the bag, then it was tied, and I was left in this state until we reached Penzance. Before the crew left the train they took me into the main dining saloon and tied the bag with rope to one of the tables. Then they all wished me good night and off they went home.

I could feel the train going slowly back to the sidings at Ponsandane. Remember that this was only my second day at work. It was no good – the tears had to flow, first a trickle, then a flood. I could move around in my bag – there seemed to be plenty of room. I could also taste mustard – I put my hand up to my hair and could feel it plastered down with all sorts of muck. By this time I started to tremble. I felt cold. I think I was in shock! Thank goodness I was on my own in the bag as I started to wet myself – the shame of it! By this time, I was quite sure I would be found dead. It would be in next week's *Cornishman* of course. The headline would read 'Railway Boy Found Dead In

Bag'. I would become famous, if only for one edition. I had no sense of time. I started to feel sick. I think it must have been the smell from all the rubbish. By now the tears were in full flood.

Then in the distance I could hear voices. It was the cleaners working their way through the train. I started to shout, but to no avail. Then they were in the restaurant car.

'What the bloody hell is this, Sid?'

'Could be a dead sheep,' said Sid. 'You know what funny buggers these dining car blokes are, Jack.'

After a short pause Jack replied. 'Come on, my ansom, what would they want with a dead sheep in a bag?'

I was beginning to think that two madmen had arrived on the scene.

'It's not a sheep – it's me!' I shouted.

'Stand back,' said Sid. 'It might be violent!'

After a moment Jack said, 'Sounds like a child to me.'

With that one of them undid the rope and the bag fell about me.

'Some bugger will pay for this,' one of them said as he pulled me out. I must have been a sorry sight, for the look of concern on both of their faces was genuine. The only bonus of this sorry tale was that one of the crew had thought to leave the dreaded page boy uniform on one of the seats, so I was spared the indignity of trying to go home with no clothes on.

'What crew did this to you, my ansom?' asked Jack.

I told him that it was the Cornish crew, and a look of relief came over his face.

'Well that's all right then. At least it wasn't them bloody emmets.'

After all the excitement of my initiation I felt quite exhausted and decided not to go home straight away. Instead I walked up Causeway Head, bought sixpence-worth of chips and ate them as I walked. I wandered down

Chapel Street, past the Egyptian building with its columns and vivid decorations on the right-hand side, and further down on the left I passed the Admiral Benbow with its colourful frontage. I was soon on the Promenade walking past the War Memorial, and found myself at the Battery Rocks. I sat there and looked out over the bay. As always the magic of that place started to work and I could feel the tensions and the hurt of that day slipping from me. Soon I was my old self again.

Although somewhat overwhelmed by the initiation I could now start to see the funny side of it. I expect it happened to all the boys when they started work on the diners, and I would not be treated differently from any of the others. It was something we all had to go through. These sort of things did happen in life. I remembered Mr Elwood, one of the teachers, telling us about the blooding that took place at a youngster's first fox hunt. A most terrifying experience, and I felt sure that the image of such a happening would come back and haunt them for years to come.

The feeling of nausea that had been with me since my time in the bag returned, and I tried to find a place where I could be sick in private. Afterwards I felt quite spent. Soon I started to feel a chill; I sat on the rocks and wrapped my arms around my knees, which were drawn up to my chin. As always here the time flew by, and before I knew it I could see the *Scillonian* coming across the bay from the direction of Mousehole on its return run from the Isles of Scilly. It must now have been about 7.30pm. Had I really been here all that time? I was beginning to understand what Mr Hitchings, my old headmaster, meant when he told May, my stepmother, that I was prone to living in a world of my own. I would have agreed, if asked, that this indeed was the case. After all, if you lived in a world of your own you could not be hurt by others, and I tended to wrap my solitude about me like a protective cloak.

The fact that I had not been home from work yet would mean nothing. At Alverne Buildings there were so many of us that one could easily be gone for some considerable time without any of the other folk even realising it. This fact meant a free hand to me, and I would wonder off quite happily on my own.

As a child one of my favourite walks was over to Newlyn, which is still a working port, giving no concession whatever to the tourist trade, thank goodness. I used to walk up the North pier – there was so much to see. The trawlers were colourful and always busy. If the tide was out, some of the boats would lean over to such a degree that I felt sure at any moment they would fall over on their sides. However would they get them to stand upright again? If you visited on a working day you would see all sorts of exciting things going on: men mending the nets and painting the bodywork of the trawlers and more than likely a man welding, the sparks dancing off the metal like a sparkler on November the Fifth.

If you walked about halfway up the pier you would see little terns always trying to scratch a living, and always in great rush. There was always the smell of tar and diesel oil, and at the very end there was some thick rope kept under the shelter. It was here that I would have a look over the edge. Sometimes fish would be swimming about. Quite often a small van or car would come up the pier and turn round at the very end, having delivered something to one of the vessels. I felt sure that one of them would land up in the water, but they never did.

One day I was walking back down the pier and came upon some visitors. There was father, mother and two children, a boy of about nine and a girl of about 11. The father had been fishing and had just landed a pollack. It looked so helpless thrashing about on the floor. There was much excitement, but I took note that it was only the girl who was getting hysterical.

'Kill it, daddy, kill it!'

She was jumping up and down, and she must have repeated these words at least twenty times. I felt quite sure that if her father had given her the 1950s equivalent of a 'My Little Pony Abattoir Set' for Christmas she would have been overjoyed...

Such were memories going through my mind as I sat on my rock.

The next day I was off to London again, then the next day back home to Cornwall. I could rest assured that with my initiation behind me, I had nothing to fear. Trusting youth! How more wrong could I be? As we passed Camborne, one of the lads grabbed me and dragged me screaming into the vestibule again. He let the leather window strap down and pushed my head out of the window. There was nothing I could do, as he was much stronger than me. After a few seconds I could feel wet on my face. I closed my eyes and prayed that the torment would soon be over. It was only after my head was pulled back in that I had any idea what had taken place. I spotted one of the kitchen lads doing up his flies. The rest was left to my imagination. It is with relief that I can tell you that after this I was left well alone, and indeed I was to see others suffer the same as I had. That is how things were done in a man's world.

3
DORIS, DENTURES AND DIGS

As far as I am aware, I was quite privileged to be allowed to do the 'calling in' on the 'Limited'. I am informed that on other trains it was either the conductor or the attendants who called passengers in for meals; I know for a fact that on the 'Royal Duchy' the pantry boy never did it. To he honest, it gave me some grand feeling of superiority, and on many occasions I would put on a very affected accent, but should some passenger ask me a question while I was calling in, I would forget myself and answer in broad Cornish.

On other occasions I would do it with a severe stammer. The first time I tried this I found that it took twice as long, and when I got back to the car I had a right telling off from the conductor. It rather depended on which film I had seen the previous evening. If the mood took me I would do it as Elvis with a Southern States drawl. As I pushed the door open I would also give a swing of the hip, but decided to stop doing this after getting some very strange looks from some sailors on their way home for the weekend. One day I even did it like Charles Laughton in *The Hunchback of Notre Dame* – one eye half closed and dragging one of my legs. On another occasion I did it as the Tin Man from *The Wizard Of Oz*, walking as if all my joints were stiff. But I think my very best was Robert Newton in *Treasure Island*. This was really over the top, but at

least I could use my Cornish accent. What the passengers thought of such antics, I have no idea. At the very least they must have thought that I was on day release from the local Home For The Bewildered.

At that time, we had lady cleaners who travelled with the guard, and one of their chores was the cleaning of the lavatories. One fateful day will ever stay imprinted in my memory, and even after all these years I recall it with a feeling of slight panic. The name of the cleaner on this particular day was Mary. She was a nice person, always friendly and something of a mother figure to me and the other youngsters in our crew. If there was a cut to be tended, she was always ready with the iodine and a bandage. She was always dressed in a blue wrap-around apron that was so popular at the time.

I had not been working long and it was the first time I had been allowed to do the calling in. Summoning up all the courage I could, off I set in my dreaded page boy's uniform feeling very nervous of the task ahead. Sliding the first compartment door open I announced, 'The second sitting for tea, please.'

And so I went on my way. After doing two or three coaches I saw the blue of Mary's apron. She was a nice person, and not too upset by a little familiarity, so I threw myself at her, grabbing her waist with one hand and slapping her bottom with the other. At the same time, I gave

The style and comfort of a GWR restaurant car is clearly seen here in the SVR's preserved example. Although there was an impression of spaciousness, things were rather more cramped than they appeared. *David Harvey*

her a huge kiss on the cheek. You can imagine my horror when, after a few seconds, the knowledge dawned that this person was not in fact our Mary. There before me stood a woman wearing a blue coat; a woman of commanding and awesome stature. I think it was the pince-nez that added to her air of grandeur.

'Young man!' she exclaimed. 'What do you think you are doing? I happen to be a First Class passenger!'

By this time I was in severe shock. 'Sorry, madam,' I replied. 'I thought you were the lavatory woman.'

The screech she gave was like an alarm bell, which should have warned me that the whole sorry story would not stay a secret for long as off I went to do the rest of the calling in. As you can guess, it was not long after my return to the restaurant car that the conductor had a little chat with me. The next day I was called into head office and was suspended from duty for three days.

There were many duties that I was requested to perform while we were stationed at Paddington station awaiting the down trip. One of these was to go to the linen room to collect the newly laundered tablecloths, the waistcoats and 'monkey jackets' for the attendants, and the clean cloths for the kitchen staff. The linen rooms were situated on platform 1 next to the administrative offices for the dining cars.

Working in the linen rooms were four

very formidable women. One of them was Irish and had such a heavy accent that I could make nothing of what she said. Another had such a bad stammer that I could make nothing of what she said either. The third always seemed to be in a bad temper, and would say, 'If only it were Friday', as if this statement would somehow make everything fine. But it was number four that really terrified me. Doris, the lady in question, was huge, but to be fair, like many such ladies, she was always very jolly. She would frequently make a lunge at me, and on one occasion managed to capture me.

'Come here, my lovey, there's a speck of dust from that dirty old engine on your pretty face.'

She then took out her huge hanky, spat on it, and proceeded to wipe it all over my face. Like most youngsters of that age I was to take advantage of her affection for me, and I can assure you that when I was made up to attendant, my waistcoat and jacket were the cleanest and best pressed in the whole of the Western Region. I will concede that standing next to Doris was rather like standing next to a very friendly octopus, but this was a small price to pay.

The Friday woman could not have been more different; all I can say is that, if she had lived in India, she would have been sacred. When my octopus was on holiday, I was in for a very lean time.

'Can't wrap me around your finger like you do Doris, young man…'

Her linen order was always wrong and I prayed for the time to go by so that my Doris would return.

One day, waiting for our order to be put up, I sat on a chair and Doris came and sat on top of me. When she finally moved the circulation had gone from my legs. It was some time before I could stand up, let alone move.

I always found it strange that her husband was such a tiny man of about 8

stone. I met him once, when he came in with a sick note for the office. It was the time when she was having her veins done. He told me she was a magic dancer, very light on her feet, and they had met at a dance just after the war. They had been happily married ever since.

Doris was a smashing person and over the years I was to grow very fond of her. She always brought her holiday photos in for me to see, and at Christmas she always gave me a card. The friendship lasted until I left British Railways, and the day I told her I was going she grabbed me and almost squeezed me to death. Even after I had left, I would call and have a chat if I was near Paddington, and did so for quite a few years. The last time I called to see her the staff told me that she and her husband had retired and gone down to Dawlish to live. They also told me me that her husband had once been a very good boxer. Such happy memories…

One day a party of about 20 old folk from the East End of London were returning on the 'Limited' from Cornwall after a holiday in St Ives, and we had 20 places reserved for them for tea in the Third Class saloon. They were a very happy crowd and there was an atmosphere of fun about them. One of them told me that 12 of them had never had a holiday until now. They all thought St Ives was wonderful and they would all be saving up like mad for another holiday there as soon as it could be arranged. It was great to see them all. What a life they had – many of them had lost loved ones in the Blitz. They all said they thought the Cornish accent was great fun, so then the lads decided to lay it on thick – it was 'ansom' this and 'ansom' that!

When we were approaching Southall in West London after they had had their tea, there was a panic. We were clearing the tables of the tea things and putting the dirty tablecloths into the bag to be

Another view of the 'Limited' behind a 'King', this time No 6024 *King Edward I*. Happily, this locomotive is now preserved. *Lens of Sutton*

returned to the linen room. One old lady had taken out her dentures to enable her to cope with the sandwiches and had put them under her serviette for safe keeping. After tea she went to the toilet and on her return found that the tables had been cleared.

'Er, mate…' she said to me, while trying to cover her mouth with her hand. 'My gnashers 'ave gone. What a bleedin' carry on!'

I told her not to worry and I was sure we would be able to find them. All of her party thought it very funny, and helped me and the other lads to tip all the linen out of the bags.

'My old man'll go mad if I go 'ome without 'em.'

Unfortunately they could not be found and that was that. I told her that if we found them we would write to her, and I took down her address.

'Cor blimey, mate, I don't 'alf feel daft!' she said.

'Don't worry, Ada, you can borrow a spare set o' mine,' her friend Elsie told her.

'Come off it, Elsie – my mouth ain't as big as yours, and that's a fact, mate!'

At this remark, all the others hooted with laughter.

That evening I did not go back to Old Oak Common with the train but spent about an hour and a half in the linen room, emptying all the bags out. At last I found the teeth; they were the old Bakelite type. The office wrote to Ada, and a few days later as I was walking up number 2 platform at Paddington, carrying some clean tablecloths piled so high that I could hardly see over the top of them, all of a sudden I felt someone pinch my backside. I turned quickly and there was Ada and her husband.

'Thanks, mate,' said her husband. 'Her 'ead's as empty as a eunuch's underpants, and that's a fact!'

Ada smiled at me and I could see that

her teeth were in their rightful place. 'Hope to see you again, cock. Take care,' she said.

I did indeed see her again many times. The holiday to St Ives became an annual event, and the drama of the teeth was repeated many times by Ada.

Of course, all these journeys to and from London required an overnight stay in the capital, and as you can imagine the quality of accommodation was most important when working away from home; it was essential to have a good night's rest. In those days most of the digs available in London were in Wells House Road, at the back of Old Oak Common Lane. In other words, they were just across the way from the railway sidings, making them most convenient. Good digs were like gold dust, and once found had to be kept at all costs.

Mrs Nancy Hines was to become my landlady; a widow in her early 30s with two small sons, she had a reputation of being a bit of a stickler. Originally she had come up from Somerset, and had all the hallmarks of a country girl. In all the years I knew her I don't think I ever saw her wear make-up; she was quite tall and slim with a healthy complexion. She had high cheek bones and flawless skin, and always stood erect; even when she sat down it was always on a high dining chair. She never seemed to relax. Even after closing time she was always busy. I have never known a woman darn so many clothes.

Apparently her husband had been killed in an accident on the railway and, try as you might, she would never talk about him. It was almost as if her silence would somehow protect her from the hurt of his untimely death. The sadness of her past never really left her and sometimes, when the shield of protection slipped, a glance would show the pain within. She once told me that it was not carrying the cross in life that hurt, it was the splinters from it. How right she was. She was very proud of her two boys, and rightly so – they were smashing children, although we never saw much of them, as they were usually in bed when we went in at night, and were still in bed when we left in the morning. Nancy fashioned her hair in a bun most of the time and always wore a wrap-around apron with a floral print. Her hands always appeared to be sore from the constant washing of dishes, clothes and sheets.

Her house was a semi, not very grand but spotless. The long narrow kitchen had a glass roof and when it rained the noise was quite considerable. The dining room led off from the kitchen and backed on to the lounge. There was a downstairs front bedroom where the two boys slept. Upstairs there was a front bedroom where Nancy slept, and this was always kept locked. A middle bedroom had a double bed in it, and finally there was a small back bedroom with two single beds, the space between them being minute.

Although spotless, the house was never warm and in the winter it was usual to sleep not only in your underwear, but also with an overcoat on top of the bed. Nancy supplied a pair of sheets, one pillow and two thin blankets. We often woke to find ice on the inside of the window in winter. The only exception to this was the lounge, where in the winter there was always a coal fire burning. I think Nancy got some coal from British Railways as part of her pension.

Looking back now, I would call the furnishings sparse. The furniture was of a solid utilitarian quality, mass-produced after the war – functional but not elegant. On the table there was always a thin plastic tablecloth with no particular pattern on it, just a swirl of colour. The chairs were ladder-backed, and the floor was covered with lino that had a dark gold motif. On the wall were the then

fashionable three china ducks, evenly spaced out, giving the impression that they might take off at any moment. The light in the middle of the room never seemed to be not strong enough, and there was always a dimness. The small two-seater settee was dark red in colour, and no one ever sat on it. The two wooden-framed pictures on the wall were of country scenes; I always thought they were a concession to Nancy's rural past. Above the fireplace, there was a mirror, and a fine Bush radio stood in the corner, although I can never remember hearing it work.

The lavatory was at the back of the house behind the kitchen; there wasn't one upstairs. You could have the use of a chamber pot, but if you used it you would have to empty it in the morning, then wash it out, using the tap in the back yard. In the lavatory there was no toilet paper as we know it today, just pieces of newspaper threaded on to a piece of string. There were some well worn towels to use but only ever cold water. The cost of a night's accommodation was 5 shillings, which also covered the cost of a cup of tea. The cups and saucers were in mid-green, of a pattern that must have been in use in millions of homes up and down the country.

There were two of us off the 'Limited' using these digs, as well as a lad off the 'Duchy' and another lad from an unnamed train from Plymouth. I don't think we ever met all at the same time because of the different shift arrangements.

Nancy was not a bad woman. She was like we all were in those days, possessing very little so having to make sure that her home was not abused in any way. As I came to know her better, we had long talks about all sorts of things, but I always felt that there was an invisible shield about her, and no matter how long I knew her I was unable to reach the depths of her personality. When I was foolish enough to give her a Christmas or birthday card, the shield would come up very quickly and slam in your face.

On only one occasion was I to see the shield slip. Awaking one morning about 2 o'clock, I looked out of the bedroom window and, because of the glass roof, I could see that there was a light on in the kitchen. Thinking we had been broken into, I crept downstairs, but when I looked into the lounge there was Nancy. I had never seen her like this before. She was sitting on a stiff high-backed chair, wearing a towelling dressing gown over her nightdress. She had let her hair down and it was beautiful, resting in waves on her shoulders, and as she moved her head there was a sheen to it. She was crying. What on earth was the matter? There I stood, a mere teenager in my striped pyjamas with a white cord about my waist, nothing on my feet. After what seemed like ages to me, I was able to see the cause of the tears. She opened her right hand and revealed two whitlows, both inflamed and sore. It was not uncommon to have whitlows in those days – most of us had them. Fresh fruit was not readily available, and even when the market had some, how could any of us afford to buy it? Consequently we were not getting enough vitamins.

I then did something that I had never done before, and never did again. I made her a cup of tea. She sat there, with her head in her hands. I put the cup before her and there we sat, drinking our tea. There were a few more sobs from Nancy but nothing was said. When we had finished she stood up and went through to the kitchen, took two aspirins and put the light out. As she came back in I stood up, then as she came to walk past me I put my arms about her, kissed her cheek and let my hand run down that glorious hair. She rested her head on my shoulder only for

an instant. It was a slow hand that pushed me from her and, when I looked, she was the colour of crimson..

Being only a teenager I was overcome with embarrassment and looked at the floor. It was just at that moment that we heard a noise. It was water – but where was it coming from?

Nancy said, 'It's not raining, is it?'

I shook my head. Like two fugitives we crept into the kitchen in silence. She did not put on the light, but picked up a torch. We crept into the back yard, and when we were in the middle she pointed the torch in the direction of the noise. Would you believe it? There was the lad off the Plymouth train relieving himself out of the bedroom window and on to the kitchen roof. It was not to happen a second time!

One day one of the lads came to work and told us the astounding news that, at the Metropolitan variety theatre in Edgware Road, they had a show with some moving female nudes. He had seen a billboard advertising it in Praed Street. After thinking about it, for about a second and a half, we all decided to go and have a look. It is the only time that I can remember the whole crew, including the conductor, going out en bloc.

We were, however, in for a disappointment. Yes, they had nudes, but they stood still on a dais, and this moved, not the girls. What a con! Never mind. It was more than a boy of 16 had seen before.

While we were at the theatre I noticed that the next week they had Max Miller topping the bill. When I arrived back at the digs I did not tell Nancy what I had seen, but I did tell her about Max Miller. Most unusually for her, she said that her late husband had liked him very much and thought him to be very funny. Then I made the suggestion that I would take her to see him. She came out with a whole string of reasons why she could not go. Who would look after the boys? After much discussion, including a trip by me to her friend next door to ask if she could babysit, and on the understanding that we would go to the first house so that we could be back at a reasonable time, she eventually said yes. She had never been to a theatre in London, and we went on the Friday of the following week.

When our train pulled in on platform 8 there she was. She looked very nervous, and when I stepped down from the train she appeared visibly relieved. As it was winter, she was wearing a dark grey overcoat with six large shiny buttons on the front, and when she turned I saw that there was a small piece of material across the small of her back. This also had two shiny buttons on either side. Her small hat was a lighter shade of grey and it had a small feather in it, secured in place with a gold bead. On her feet she wore sturdy brown shoes, which must have cost her many clothing coupons. Around her neck was a string of small pearls, and under this a lilac blouse and a thin cardigan. She wore no make-up, or was it just possible that I could see a touch of rouge? In her hand she had a brown handbag, which was very shiny, not unlike the one I had seen our young Queen carrying in the *Illustrated London News*. I could smell 'Lily of the Valley'. We went into number 8 refreshment rooms and had a pot of tea for two and some scones. It was still only 5.00pm.

When we came out of the station we turned left into Praed Street, walked past St Mary's Hospital on the left then the News Theatre on our right. As soon as it was possible I went into the Metropolitan and bought us two good tickets for the show, in the stalls. We still had some time before it started, so we went into a pub. She told me that it was the first time she had been in a pub with a man who was not her husband. I ordered her a gin and orange and had half a pint of Red Barrel. Nancy sat bolt upright. There was to be no lowering of her defences this evening.

Later we walked over the road and into the theatre, taking our seats early. As we passed the bar, which was at the back of the stalls, we could see a blue haze of smoke coming from it. The seats were comfortable in deep red velvet. About halfway up each side of the stage there were two oblong boxes, and around these there were little golden lights; I explained to Nancy that when the show started, a number would appear in these boxes, which would correspond with the number of the act in the programme so one would know who was on stage.

The orchestra entered the pit, people were now filling up the seats very quickly, and it was not long before the show started. As the curtain went up, we saw nine chorus girls kicking their legs above their heads – it was amazing. As the show went on, we saw some trick cyclists, roller-skaters, a magician, and finally a dog act. When one of the dogs relieved himself against the curtain, everyone was in stitches. In the interval we kept our seats and saw the safety curtain come down, advertising Craven 'A' cigarettes.

The second half started with a singer, then it was time for the great man himself. When the curtain went back the 'Cheeky Chappie' was standing in the middle of the stage with the microphone in front of him. He was wearing a silk suit with printed pansies all over it. The audience went mad. It took some time before he could start, and when he did, it was magic. There were all the usual innuendos – his timing was perfect.

'Now, love. Stop it or you'll get me into trouble.' Much laughter. 'Now here's a funny one. This is a funny one.' All the women threw up their hands in mock horror; even our Nancy was laughing her head off. I had never seen her like this before. It was said that Max Miller was 'The Pure Gold of Music Hall', and I am sure they were right.

When the show was over we went to a cafe. Nancy had scrambled egg and I had beans on toast. We then took the train to East Acton and walked home. As we were going along, she asked me if, next day when I was at Paddington, I could get a copy of *Picture Post* for her, as the little man who kept the corner shop had run out and she did so like to keep up with the news.

4
A WHOLE NEW WORLD

The most important element in the running of a dining car was timing, without which all was lost. It was absolutely imperative for it to all go like clockwork. Each member of the crew had certain duties to perform and in the right sequence.

First there was the obligatory glass of tea to start the day. The kitchen staff started on board earlier than the saloon staff by an hour or so. The attendant's first job was to lay the tables for lunch, because there was not time to do this after two sittings of coffee. You can imagine that when I first started work as a lad I found the laying of the tables bewildering, all those implements that had to be laid out in a particular order. There were cruet sets, consisting of a tray with containers of salt, pepper and mustard and a handle to pick it up. The pantry boy had to make sure both salt and pepper were topped up at all times. The mustard, Colman's, was made up fresh every day. If any cruets had a dull tarnish on them, they had to be cleaned by soaking them for a minute in a bowl of boiling water with some raw soda added. This was a very dangerous thing to do, and it was usual to use a fork to lift them out. This done, they were rinsed off in hot water, which assured a right good shine. They would come up like new and there, resplendent, was the 'GWR' motif on the handle. The same system was used for all the plated utensils. The teapots came up especially well and when in use looked a treat. When one inspector told me that mine were the best kept on the whole of the Western Region, I was overjoyed and almost burst with pride.

Another of my specialities were the drinking glasses. They had to be sparkling. The greatest sin to commit as a pantry boy was to allow a glass or cup to be used with lipstick on it. The conductor took a very dim view of this and showed his displeasure when the time came to split the tips at the end of the day. In fact, a good pantry boy was a great asset to the crew; should you go sick, which was not often, there was a lot of groaning. It meant that the attendants had to do the washing up. How sad!

Not long after I started as a pantry boy I recall walking from the saloon back to pantry and being stopped by the conductor.

'Why have you nothing in your hand?' he asked.

I said that I did not know what he meant.

He pointed to an empty tray on a table. 'You see that tray, son? You could have brought that back with you. Always make sure your brains do the thinking and your feet do the walking.'

It was advice that I was to put to good use over the years. In fact, I was to remember his words one Saturday when I was working the 'Duchy' on a down trip.

GREAT WESTERN RAILWAY.
RESTAURANT CAR CONDUCTOR'S REPORT.

In reply to your ____ (45-1)

In your reply please quote ____

From CONDUCTOR. Williams
Plymouth 3 — Car No. 9675
Jan 14 1947

To R.P.P. Setterfield Esq
Paddington

Sir

On the above date AH Salt, caught his hand in the door of the kitchen hotplate, badly cutting and bruising his middle finger. He left the train at Exeter, to get his hand dressed. He came to the car this morning 16/1. and is unable to work. and handed me a doctors certificate

Your Obedient Servant
G Williams

250 pads, 100 lvs.—B.M./17. 1940 (S)

Above Absence through sickness or injury was rare, despite restaurant car kitchens being fairly dangerous places to work. This conductor's report records that attendant Salt 'caught his hand in the door of the kitchen hotplate, badly cutting and bruising his middle finger. He left the train at Exeter to get his hand dressed. He came to the car this morning and is unable to work and handed me a doctor's certificate.' Note how in the 1940s a conductor would address his boss as 'Your obedient servant'! *Author's collection*

Left A view along the central aisle of the saloon. One day I was so busy trundling up and down that I rubbed the skin off my toes. On the advice of an old porter I soaked my feet in permanganate of potash, which did the trick! *David Harvey*

The conductor that day was Freddie Greville, and it was the only day when I can remember doing five – yes, *five* – sittings of tea. When we got off the train at Penzance I found a platform trolley, sat on it and took the shoe off my right foot. It was squelching in blood. I had done that much rushing around that I had taken the skin off four toes. I went off, and on the advice of an old porter soaked my feet in permanganate of potash. After this treatment my feet were as tough as camels' tongues! That day I earned the most I ever did in the way of tips for one day – £5.

As well as setting up the catering, there was our own toilet to see to. I well remember looking over to the kitchen and seeing Ernie Keneally preparing to shave. He would spend what seemed like hours rubbing a razor-blade inside a smooth tumbler to sharpen it. I also remember seeing Jack Harper looking into a mirror each morning and applying mascara to his moustache. Or seeing Jack Pascoe putting lather on his face and wanting to use the comfort of my pantry, because it was nice and warm.

Indeed, when I worked on the trains I was never cold. Unlike the present-day InterCity 125 diesels, where the engine and coaches form a permanently coupled unit, in those days in Penzance at 5.00am one of the staff would start up the oil-fired boiler situated at the eastern end of the platforms at the station. This would eventually distribute steam to all the platforms and, via pipes, to the locomotive-less coaches, thus preheating them prior to departure. I say eventually as I am informed that the pump tended to be a little temperamental. It was fascinating to see the steam escaping and rising in clouds when there were no coaches present; the original feeder pipe can still be seen today.

I can never remember the weather being so severe that we had to cancel a train. Until 1958 the inland Teign Valley route in Devon was very useful as an alternative whenever storms made the Dawlish seawall section impassable. However, owing to the nature of the Teign Valley line and its difficult curves, the main-line engine would have to be replaced by two smaller 'Bulldog' Class locomotives at either Exeter or Newton Abbot, depending on the direction of travel. These were used until the train rejoined the main line.

One day my good friend Les Pender was working the 'Cornishman' from Penzance to Wolverhampton, and when they got to Newton Abbot they were informed that the seawall was down at Dawlish, and they were diverted on to the Teign line. What a sight the 'Cornishman' must have been on its stately journey through all the small stations to Exeter. The branch was 17 miles in length, and like so many others it did not survive Dr Beeching's axe. It started life in 1882 and closed to passenger traffic in 1958. However, it managed to survive for goods traffic until 1967, then sadly it was the end. After closure, diverted trains went via Okehampton and Lydford Junction on the old Southern Railway route between Plymouth and Exeter.

Back on the 'Limited', Dickie Mitchell often asked me to clean his shoes for a threepenny piece. I would do this instead of eating my breakfast, and if some of the other attendants felt lazy I would clean their shoes for the same fee. Some days I started off with over a shilling in my pocket – wealth indeed! It must be said that all this activity quite often took place without the presence of the conductor. It depended on the individual. Some conductors would join the staff at the sidings and have breakfast with the rest of the crew, but if they were the London-based 'Limited' crew the conductor would quite often join the train at Paddington station. The London crew were 'Limited 1' and the Cornish crew 'Limited 2'. Quite a good deal of friendly rivalry existed between the two crews. After I passed the pantry boy stage and became an attendant, I was transferred from the Cornish 'Limited' to the London one, and my wages went up correspondingly from £2 5s to £7. The day that happened I thought I was a millionaire!

One day, when all the chores were done, we started to move out of the carriage shed at Old Oak Common, at walking pace as usual to negotiate the extensive sidings, and when we were clear of the shed, but not clear of the siding, there was a slight bump, and we found ourselves at a 20 per cent list. We had become derailed, the one and only time this happend to me. A few plates fell and broke, and the cupboard in which the ice was kept came open and its contents spilled on the floor. In the kitchen quite a lot of vegetables were thrown about.

One of the lads – I cannot remember which, except that it was one of the attendants – suddenly appeared with two empty wine bottles. He then took from the drinks cupboard three-quarters of a bottle of scotch and poured it into one of the wine bottles, then did the same with a bottle of gin. He told me to stand back, then broke the two original spirit bottles by hitting them against the sink.

RESTAURANT CAR MEALS SERVED. (7294)

Birkenhead 2 Car. *July* 193*7* *alternate days.*

Dept. *Paddn 9.10am*   Arr. *B'head 1.54pm.*
" *B'head 11.55am.*   " *Paddn. 6.5pm.*

Date	Breakfasts 3/6 and over	Over 2/- to 3/5	2/- and under	Luncheons 2/6	3/-	3/6	Teas	Dinners 5/-	3/6	A la Carte	Suppers	Sandwiches
1												
2												
3												
4												
5				23	8		48					
6	23	6	4	2	1		2					10
7				24	9		48					
8	15	3	4	7	3		9					
9				19	8		5					
10	8	2		23	17		4					2
11												
12				32	11		36					
13	23	4	5	3	2		2					
14				21	6		23					
15												

Above and right Detailed records had to be kept of meals served as well as expenditure and receipts. The record of meals served refers to a Birkenhead-Paddington service of 1937 running on alternative days (except Sunday), hence the serving of breakfasts only every other day. The large sheet records expenditure and receipts on the 'Limited' month by month in the early 1950s. *Author's collection*

20 CAR Limited 1.

Forward Journey 10.30 am Paddington to Penzance } Alternate
(503) Return " 9.45 am Penzance to Paddington } days

MONTH	1951			1952			1953			1954		
	Receipts	Expenditure	Gross Profit % of Receipts	Receipts	Expenditure	Gross Profit % of Receipts	Receipts	Expenditure	Gross Profit % of Receipts	Receipts	Expenditure	Gross Profit % of Receipts
	£	£		£	£		£	£		£	£	
PROVISIONS.												
January	861	422	50.99	1,052	515	51.05	788	362	54.06	885	352	60.23
February	674	340	49.56	747	361	51.67	653	301	53.91	745	307	58.79
March	1,245	543	56.39	1,051	424	59.66	881	428	51.42	813	359	55.84
April	1,211	619	48.89	1,326	553	58.30	1,212	562	53.63	1,164	441	62.11
May	1,244	654	47.43	1,268	556	56.15	1,208	573	52.57	972	361	62.86
June	1,543	748	51.52	1,430	604	57.76	976	554	43.24	971	387	60.14
	6,778	3,326	50.93	6,874	3,013	56.17	5,718	2,780	51.38	5,550	2207	
July	1,582	774	61.07	1,331	605	54.55	1,251	625	50.04	1,179	508	56.91
August	1,689	800	52.63	1,330	507	61.88	1,556	672	56.81	1,491	555	62.78
September	1,693	723	57.29	1,582	619	60.87	1,282	486	62.09	1,449	524	63.84
October	1,253	605	51.72	1,305	525	59.77	1,179	439	62.77	1,399	473	66.19
November	859	439	48.89	819	320	60.93	862	290	66.36	1,059	390	63.17
December	921	494	46.36	876	444	49.32	976	385	60.55			
TOTAL	14,775	7,161	51.53	14,117	6,033	57.26	12,824	5,677	55.73			
WINES, SPIRITS, CIGARS, &c.												
January	227	126	44.59	303	165	45.54	181	95	47.51	252	144	42.86
February	185	107	42.16	197	119	39.59	177	95	46.33	233	129	44.64
March	288	161	44.10	271	143	47.23	207	114	44.93	210	165	22.38
April	265	148	44.15	302	170	43.71	283	160	43.46	273	149	54.75
May	267	151	43.45	309	184	40.45	276	156	43.48	238	144	39.50
June	304	156	48.68	276	152	44.93	198	87	56.06	207	114	44.93
	1,536	849	44.73	1,658	933	43.73	1,322	707	46.52	1,413	823	
July	285	157	44.91	270	148	45.19	246	154	37.40	266	150	43.61
August	287	163	43.24	233	131	44.63	367	231	37.06	303	185	38.94
September	331	179	45.92	277	149	46.21	304	198	34.87	329	195	40.73
October	318	161	49.37	276	149	46.01	303	173	42.90	313	181	42.17
November	271	149	45.02	211	121	42.65	242	139	42.56	253	145	42.69
December	264	164	37.88	256	147	42.58	285	175	38.60			
TOTAL	3,292	1,822	44.65	3,181	1,783	43.95	3,069	1,777	57.91			

'Leave them as they are, son,' he instructed, as he disappeared with the booty. Sure enough, in due course, along came a travelling inspector and asked if there had been any damage. We merely pointed at the evidence on the floor and shook our heads. Later that day a relief train took our place, while we had to wait several hours before we travelled 'light' (that is with no passengers) from Paddington to Penzance. Still, we did have a drink or two to help pass the time.

On Fridays on the up 'Royal Duchy' this corridor would be packed with sailors on weekend leave. They would be looking for the bar and would be disappointed that there was only a restaurant car. *David Harvey*

That story of drink reminds me of a later occasion when I was working the 'Royal Duchy'. One of the attendants was Charlie Richards, who, poor man, had much to bear. At some time in the past he had had a terrible stomach operation, although it seems he outlived most of his colleagues. The kitchen boy that day was my friend Les Pender; he was a well-built lad and always game for a laugh. It transpired that on that particular day, when we got to Plymouth on the up trip, there were hundreds of sailors going home on weekend leave. As we only had a restaurant car and not a bar, if they wanted a drink they would have to buy a meal first. After the meal, if we did not want the tables for tea, we would let them drink all the way to Paddington.

After the sailors had had a few drinks, Charlie put it to them that in fact our Les could drink any of them under the table, and he was only 17. This was greeted with a lot of back-slapping and laughter. The outcome was that they took Charlie at his word, and the bet was on. I poured cold tea into the glass that Les was to use, and Charlie put his finger into some rum and rubbed it around the top of the glass. To prevent the glasses getting mixed up, the sailors' glasses were kept at the other end of the pantry.

Young, Les did us proud that day. On the way back to Old Oak Common we split the spoils between us, and later departed to a pub to have a real drink. Les and I have been friends all these past years and we still are.

The public were also not beyond taking advantage of the system. I am reliably informed that after the war, when china for the home was in short supply, all one had to do was to go to St Erth station and travel the relatively short distance to Penzance and you could obtain enough of it to keep you going for some years. On the way down from Paddington people would dash off and purchase a beverage from the various refreshment rooms en route, which were served in china cups. By the time St Erth was reached there were so many cups under foot on the train that it was a job to sit down. Mind you, they all had the GWR logo on them, although that was nothing to worry about; if asked, you could say that it stood for Granny's Wartime Requisition, and I am sure that would have been the end of the matter. One can almost imagine father, mother and the kids making a day trip of it.

That reminds me of a story about one of my brothers, Tony, who was a bus conductor with the Western National bus company. As they left St Erth for Penzance he started collecting the fares from those who had just joined the bus. One formidable-looking woman said she wanted a ticket to Penzance. He told her the fare and she told him that he was wrong.

'The fare went up threepence today, my ansom,' he explained.

She was indignant. 'No it did not, young man.'

The two of them got into an argument about it, which ended with Tony saying, 'Well if you won't pay, I must ask you to get off.'

This put the tin hat on it as far as the woman was concerned. 'I will pay you, but when we get to Penzance, I will report you for being rude.'

Nothing more was said between them until they arrived at the railway station at Penzance, when Tony asked her if she would like to accompany him and the driver over to the bus depot, which was at Wherrytown, at the other end of the Promenade on the way out towards Newlyn. She said that she would. As they set off, Tony whirled his ticket machine and produced another ticket.

'That will be sixpence, please, my ansom.'

I bet her poor husband had a good ear-bashing when she returned home. Mind you, Tony's time was to come. One day, a bus he was on was going up through Market Jew Street and stopped by the post office to let some people cross the road. Tony was on the tailboard looking up at some offices where there were some pretty young ladies. Unfortunately for him, he did not see my sister-in-law, Ruby, trying to attract his attention from street level. When he walked into his house that night after work, his wife threw at him all the china they had, breaking the lot. Served him right!

One of the conductors and I had a secret, and even after all these years I do not wish to break his trust. After a few months at work, this conductor said that he would like a word with me in private, so one evening, after we had arrived at Penzance, he and I walked up the platform with the rest of the crew, but unlike them we did not leave the station. Needless to say, I wondered what he wanted me for – had I done something wrong? I would not go so far as to say that he was a great friend of mine, but to say that he was not a fair man would be doing him an injustice. After the rest of the crew had left the station, we met at the top of the stairs, where the booking office used to be in those days. He asked me if I liked my job and I said that I did. He then went on to ask me if I thought I would be on the trains for some time. I replied that this was indeed my intention.

'Look, son, I don't want you to take this the wrong way, but you don't have many clothes, do you?'

There was nothing I could say other than to agree with him.

'The evening before last I was talking to my wife about you. I was telling her of your circumstances, your wages, your home life, that sort of thing.'

He moved his weight from one foot to

the other. I looked at him but he was looking away. His body language was telling me, in no uncertain way, that he was embarrassed.

'I don't want you to be upset at what I am about to say.' After this he said nothing for some time, which made the whole thing most confusing. Time went by. We leaned on the wall, and looked back out over the station.

'Son, what I have to say to you is rather delicate.'

By now I could see our train being pulled slowly to Ponsandane, where it would spend the night. He took out a packet of Senior Service cigarettes, but did not offer me one, even though he knew I had been smoking since I was 14. Could this be the same man who clipped me about the ear for not washing my neck, or the man who said to the kitchen boy and myself, 'Fingers and feet'? We had to show him that our nails were clean, then we had to turn round and raise our shoes in turn, so he could see if they were also clean. He smoked his cigarette, looking across the station to the right where there was another entrance. Now he started rubbing his hands together, as if they were cold. This could not be the case, as it was midsummer.

'I am not trying to treat you like a child. The decision the wife and I have come to is a joint one. What I am trying to say to you is this, that in our own way we are going to try to make your lot in life a little easier.'

This last statement seemed to have taken it out of him, for he was now leaning heavily on the wall. Yet again he was looking at the other entrance. There was another long interval and nothing was said. Again out came the Senior Service. Then all of a sudden there was his wife. She walked across the front of the platforms, and as she did so she waved to us. I had met her once before on the

Promenade when the conductor and I had had the same day off and I had met them quite by chance. The three of us had sat on a seat opposite the Queens Hotel, and the conductor had wandered off to see if he could buy come ice-cream. While he was away I had asked his wife if they had any children, and she had told me that it was not possible, for medical reasons. It was just as she was coming up the stairs towards us that the penny dropped. It came to me like a thunderbolt and with so much force that my knees buckled slightly. It was now obvious that they wanted to adopt me. All of this could mean nothing else. Whatever would I say to them? 'I'm sorry but I don't think my stepmother would like it.'

'Michael,' she said. 'It's so nice to see you again.'

She gave me a hug. I was right – I had to be. Thinking to myself what a dishy foster mum she would make, the idea in some ways could have advantages. They did have a car, a Morris Oxford. He told me one day that if he was home on a Sunday they had roast beef. Now that really was something worth being adopted for. The also used real toilet paper. They must be quite well off. All this put them in a different league.

The three of us left the station, crossed the road, and walked past the Railway Hotel and up Market Jew Street. When we arrived at Colliers, the 'Fifty Shilling Tailors', he turned to me and said, 'What the wife and I would like to do is to open an account for you. You can have some new clothes and you can pay me back so much a week. What do you say?'

Well! What does one say? That I would rather have roast beef on a Sunday?

The three of us went in, and in no time at all I was fixed up with a new pair of trousers and a jacket. When I came out of the cubicle and stood in front of a full mirror, I could not believe the transformation. I could feel the tears pricking the back of my eyes. Could this really be me? In all my short life, I had never looked so grand. The male shop assistant said to the conductor's wife, 'Madam, your son does look smart.'

It was just a while before she could answer, and when she did her eyes were moist. To the conductor the man said, 'You must be very proud of him, sir.'

The conductor replied, 'I am. I am.'

I shall never forget that couple's kindness to a lad of 15, but that is how we did things in those days. When we came out of the shop the conductor told me that it was our secret, and even after 40 years it still is.

It was then that I decided I would never be short of clothes, and is perhaps the reason why I spend so much time in charity shops today!

When I walked into Alverne Buildings in my new togs, they all looked at me as if I were a stranger, and quickly came to the conclusion that I had a very good job indeed. I adored my new clothes, and at night, when I took them off, I folded the trousers into their creases and put them under my mattress to keep them well pressed. With loving care I would run my hand down the sleeves of the jacket, and I told myself that if I could save up some money from my tips I would soon have enough to buy a pair of shoes. This was a whole new world.

Another deprivation of those days was the lack of foods that today we take for granted. For example, the only time I can remember having turkey was at Christmas, and that was on the train. It was something to look forward to and I will never forget my first taste – it was heaven! What simple, uncomplicated days they were! We would hang up our sock, hole and all, on the bedpost, and if, in the morning, there were some small goodies like nuts, an orange, perhaps a penknife or a home-made catapult, you were overjoyed.

Christmas was always a problem as far as I was concerned. Until the age of about 11 I would not go to bed on Christmas Eve. Most other children went to bed, all excited about Father Christmas calling in the night. Not me! No way! The very thought of an old man with a beard coming into my room while I was asleep terrified me, and the thought that he might come down the chimney made the whole thing an utter nightmare. Had these grown-ups lost all their reasoning? Had they never heard about people like Jack the Ripper? He could be in my room, cut my throat, and be away. The grown-ups could do nothing about it. The deed would be done and I would be dead.

Another thing – they all wanted to kiss me all of a sudden. I would spend a good deal of my time wiping the spit from my cheek that all those heavy-busted aunts kept putting there. To make matters worse, they would say things like, 'Break a few hearts, that one will. You mark my words.'

So for me it was a blessing to grow up a bit, and have these unpleasant things removed from my life. I did not mind going to church at Christmas. I would be given a sixpence to put on the plate at collection time. In fact, what I would do was to make out that I was putting it into the plate with my right hand, while at the same time flicking my thumb on the base with my left hand. Even with the bit of baize on the bottom of the plate, it would still make a noise. Sixpence was half a shilling and a shilling was enough to get you into the Savoy!

The first year I was on the trains Dickie Mitch took me and the kitchen boy, both still only 15, up to Oxford Street to see the lights. For two young lads from South West Cornwall it was almost too much to take in. I pressed my nose against the window at Selfridges – I could not believe what I was seeing, for the prices on some of the toys would have kept us at home for two weeks.

There was a man selling roast chestnuts, and Dickie thought it would be a good idea to have some. Immediately the cost sprang to mind. He could tell, by the look on our faces, what we were thinking.

'It's OK, lads. They'll be treat on me.'

They were so hot. We had to keep moving them from one hand to the other so we would not get burned. They were delicious.

I was cold, but I was better off than the kitchen boy, because I was wearing the serge trousers from my uniform, which kept my legs nice and warm. I also had a pair of gloves, which the wife of one of the attendants had given me. They were a complete pair, except that one of the thumb ends was missing. It was nice of her to think of me like that.

After the chestnuts, we walked back to Edgware Road and into Praed Street, where there was a News Theatre, and Dickie treated us to a show. It lasted about an hour, during which we saw a newsreel and some cartoons. We then went on the tube train as far as East Acton, and walked to the digs from there. By this time it was starting to get late and the smog was coming in. We were soon in the thick of it and it hurt to breathe. Dickie said that we should put our hankies over our nose and mouth. He was kidding! What were hankies? As we were walking along, I told Dickie that in the morning I would clean his shoes for nothing. Then I thought better of it, and said that I would clean one for nothing. One must not be too generous. He laughed at this and patted me on the head again, like a dog. He was always doing that.

Talking of the festive season, one Christmas we arrived at Gwinear Road station in Cornwall and were told that there would be a slight delay because of snow. We all piled on to the platform and had a snowball fight, the kitchen staff against the saloon staff. We all took part, even the conductor. When the guard blew his whistle and waved his flag, we all gathered up as much snow as we could manage, and, when we were on our way again, carried on with our fight in the Third Class saloon. This was fine until the snow started to melt. Needless to say, it was down to me and the kitchen boy to mop it all up.

Another day I was watching the chef cleaning the turkey. It was huge and I was worrying that it would be too big to go into the oven. The turkey's neck, which was purple and had streaks of yellow in it, looked revolting. From the way they were behaving in the kitchen, I knew something was up. They were all whispering to one another and grinning. This was a sign for me to take care. It could be something they had in mind for me, being Christmas. But I need not have worried this time, as it was not me they were after, but Mary, the cleaning lady.

Sid the chef was sitting on the first seat in the Third Class saloon by himself. He had his head in his hands, and when Mary walked into the saloon he gave a sigh of pain and shook his head. At that point the kitchen boy gave him two aspirins with a glass of water, which he took very quickly, at the same time mopping his forehead with a kitchen towel. Mary, seeing all of this, was most concerned, and quickly sat down beside him.

'Sid, what on earth is the matter with you. You look like death,' she said.

Sid grabbed the lower region of his stomach and replied, 'Mary, I'm in agony. The pain is almost unbearable.'

To this Mary said, 'Poor you. Is it stones?'

There was silence for a few seconds, then he said, 'No, Mary. It's a man's complaint – rather delicate.'

This is how the saloon looked when the kitchen boy and I had mopped it out after our snowball fight!
David Harvey

She was not going to be outdone, and her curiosity had got the better of her.

'Sid, dear, as you know I have been married for over 30 years so you can't tell me anything to embarrass me.'

Sid gave another cringe. 'Perhaps you could take a look for me?'

She gave a nod. 'Of course, Sid, anything.'

With this he slowly lifted his apron and there it was. He had put the turkey's neck inside the fly of his check trousers. It ran down his leg for about 9 inches and was tied to his leg with a bandage. Mary went as white as a sheet, then let out a squeak, not even a scream. She shot out of her seat as if she were a cat with haemorrhoids, and ran for all her life out of the saloon. It was some time before she talked to the kitchen staff again. But much later she was to see the funny side of it, and they were forgiven.

5
ON THE 'DUCHY'

In due course I was made up to an attendant, and I worked on the 'Royal Duchy' for a while. It also ran between Paddington and Penzance, but had nothing of the image of the 'Riviera' about it. It ran later and with many more stops.

At about that time Prince Charles was at prep school at Cheam. During the school term he used to join the train every Friday evening at Newbury with his private detective, and without fail they would occupy the First Class compartment next to the restaurant car. It always amused me to think that businessmen who joining the train at Reading would find themselves in the same compartment as the future King of England. They tried to pretend that they had not seen him, and to ease their embarrassment they raised their newspapers up to their eyes, although quite often curiosity would win and they would have a peep. To me the Prince always seemed to have a sad countenance about him, and he gave me the impression of being quite nervous.

I can only remember the two of them coming into the restaurant car on one occasion. It was at the end of a very hot summer's day, and they sat down opposite one another on a table for four. It did not take me long to put a 'Reserved' card covering the two empty places. Without even acknowledging the Prince, I asked the detective if I could help.

'I would like a pot of tea for one and an orange squash.'

Off I went, and in a short time returned with the order. I put the teapot and milk in front of the detective and placed the squash in front of the Prince. The detective put his palm over the glass with the orange in it.

'How did you make this up, steward?'

I said that it was neat squash diluted with water.

He then said, 'Could you please take this away and bring a drink you can open here in front of me?'

Off I went and returned with a bottle of ginger-beer, which I opened it in front of him. He gave a nod and I poured it into a glass.

When the Prince was aboard it was almost guaranteed that we would pull into Paddington on time. As we slid into platform number 8, a Royal car would slowly come down the ramp used by the taxis. It would match our speed and come to a halt so that all the Prince had to do was to step from the train into the car and drive away.

The only other time I attended royalty was when the Duchess of Gloucester travelled between Westbury and Newbury with a friend, and I was chosen to look after them. The biggest surprise I had was when the boss told me to obtain a docket to draw three new attendants' uniforms from the stores, which were situated under number 9 platform at Paddington. I tried to explain that it was only a short time ago that I had a new uniform, but it was no good. I could not buck the system. So off I went and did as I was told. It will come as no surprise that I had to have a new shirt, new shoes, and also a haircut.

The day before they were to travel with us we had travelling down to Penzance two rolling-stock inspectors together with a dining car inspector. The next morning, when I arrived at Slopers at Ponsandane, I could not believe my eyes. The First Class compartment next to the restaurant car had almost been taken to bits, cleaned, and put back together again. All the way up to Westbury the three inspectors were edgy. When we stopped at Westbury they were waiting with the station master. As soon as the Royal party boarded the train we were on our way. I gave them about five minutes to settle themselves, and by this time the terrible three were urging me into action. I was very smart in my new clothes, and as an extra I had a pair of white gloves.

The three inspectors stood at the side of the compartment, by the outer carriage door, while I was facing the compartment, and by slightly leaning to my left I could see the trio. One was wringing his hands, another was looking at the ceiling, rocking to and fro on his heels, and the dining car inspector looked as white as a sheet. My honest opinion was that if I did not make a move they would need counselling for the rest of their lives. I tapped on the glass door, slid it open and approached the Duchess.

'Good afternoon, Your Royal Highness. Is there anything I can get you?'

She thought for a moment, then said, 'Yes. Do you think you could get me an aspirin?'

I turned to the lady travelling with her. 'Madam?' I said, and slightly moved my head towards her.

'No thank you, steward, I am quite happy, thank you.'

As I came away the three wise men were upon me, and in unison said, 'What does she want?'

By now I had the upper hand and I very slowly cleared my throat, then, taking time to adjust my tie, which did not require adjustment, said, 'A glass of water and an aspirin.'

They looked so hurt by this remark that I felt quite sorry for them.

At Newbury the Royal party departed, the journey having taken about half an hour. The three musketeers now sat down and all ordered fillet stakes with all the trimmings, washed down with a bottle of Medoc, and a brandy with their coffees, plus a cigar. The dining car inspector signed the bill, as he had done for the last two days.

Things don't change much, do they?

One day on the 'Duchy' we had this spare conductor working with us. This of course meant that the regular and relief conductors were, for some reason, unable to work, usually due to sickness or holidays. We had started the first sitting of tea and in walked a passenger, a man, wearing a winter overcoat.

'I would like some tea.'

'Please take a seat,' said the conductor. 'We will be starting the next sitting for tea in about a quarter of an hour.'

To this the man replied, 'I don't wish to wait a quarter of an hour. The place is only half full, so I will take my tea now.'

One must appreciate that to do as the man requested on a regular basis was impractical. The staff would be falling over each other and it would be chaos. So the conductor was none too pleased with the passenger's attitude.

'Very well sir. Let me take your coat.'

He took the coat and hung it on a hook at the end of the saloon. To me he said, 'Please serve this gentleman, Michael.'

Ex-GWR 'Castle' Class No 7027 *Thornbury Castle* slowly climbing towards Dainton Tunnel between Newton Abbot and Totnes with the 1.30pm Paddington-Penzance 'Royal Duchy' on 17 May 1958. *Hugh Ballantyne*

Off I went to the kitchen. 'Right away. One tea please, chef.'

The reply from the chef was something like, 'Piss off. We are in the middle of a sitting.'

The spare conductor heard this, and overruled the chef. He was indeed a brave man. The teapot was almost thrown out of the serving hatch by the kitchen staff. This particular chef wanted things his own way, as he did when the regular conductor was on duty.

'I have a mind to give the bastard the "raw soda" treatment,' he said.

What he meant by that was the placing of two or three granules of raw soda in the pot when he was making the tea. This was done only in extreme circumstances, and only by a few. While the passenger would not taste any difference, I can assure you that he would spend one day at the very least sitting in the toilet with nothing on his mind except the extreme pain in his stomach.

I took the teapot and served the man. Meanwhile the conductor walked into the pantry and dipped his hand into a tin of jam. He then walked slowly into the saloon and asked the passenger if everything was fine. The man said it was. The conductor walked to where the man's Crombie overcoat was hanging, unseen by its owner, slid his hand inside the coat, and left a considerable amount of jam on the lining. After the bill was paid, the conductor helped the man on with his overcoat, sliding his hand up and down the outside with the remark, 'What a jolly good fit.'

When I cleared his dishes from the table I noticed that our customer was a 'stiff' – in other words he had not left a tip.

'Thought he would be,' said the conductor.

A short time later the man rushed back into the saloon like a bat out of hell. He was carrying his Crombie coat, turned inside-out. He was so worked up he could not speak. He looked as if he might start to cry at any moment. He pointed to the jam.

'Well, well,' said the conductor. 'How on earth did you manage to do that?'

By this time the man had managed to reach some degree of composure. 'It was not me, you fool!'

'Was it not?'

'If you didn't put it there, how did it get there?' I thought the man was about to explode. 'If I could prove it was you, it would cost you your job. Do you hear me?'

'I have never heard anything so outrageous,' countered the conductor. 'I have worked on the trains for 20 years, and to think that after all that time anyone could say such a thing is very hurtful.'

The conductor looked as if he might be in tears at any moment. In slow motion he sat down, took out a snuff box, put some snuff up his nose and made the most incredible noise. The passenger was now completely exasperated, and seeing that he could get no further, fled the saloon.

I told the chef what I had seen and I think he was starting to see the conductor in a new light. Not such a bad chap after all.

'I can tell you this, son,' said the chef. 'That passenger won't be going to work in the morning. In a while he'll start to feel quite poorly. I hope he manages to get home in time.'

So indeed did I.

I must be very careful here not to mention any names, but if I am to tell this story I should give you the background. It is a well-known fact that the catering trade has always been very poorly paid, and indeed it was no different in the 1950s. Like most things with life, there is always a good degree of luck about what your position at work turns out to be. I had been very lucky to have been given the 'Limited' to start on; I was much more likely to earn a lot more tips than I would receive on the 'Royal Duchy', the 'Limited' being about five times busier. It was the same for the married men trying to bring up a family; the tips made up a very important part of their income.

It is a sad fact that some of the catering staff were sacked for fiddling the books. The system laid itself wide open to such abuse and, human nature being what it is, these things were sure to happen.

On some of the trains it was a case of waiting to get into dead men's shoes. If there was a vacancy on a good run, there would be many putting in for it, but if it was a train that ran at unsocial hours no one would want it.

It was quite possible to work the 'Limited' with one conductor and have a very good share-out at the end of the day. It was also possible to work the same train doing the same business and have a lousy share-out from another conductor.

On one occasion I was working with a conductor on the 'Duchy' who had a reputation for being one of the worst to work for. Violence is something that I would not associate with the dining cars in a thousand years, but on this particular evening it had all gone too far. It seems that one attendant was none too pleased with what he received in his share-out at the end of the day. We had just left Camborne on a down run, and when I went into the pantry it looked like a blood-bath – there was blood everywhere. The attendant had been so disgusted with his share that he had hit the conductor; in fact, the fight was still going on, and the chef, Les Pender and I tried to part them. In the end we succeeded.

When we got to Penzance the conductor went to the Railway Police; no charges were brought, but they were never to work the same train together again. I never saw anything like that again, thank goodness.

Talking of spare staff reminds me of an incident on a lighter note. In the corridor next to the office at Paddington was a notice board, and if the boss, Ronnie Groves, wanted anyone he would of pin a note on the board saying 'Please see me'. Such a note meant that either there was trouble or he wanted a favour. It turned out that on this occasion that it was the latter. He wanted to know if I would work a special down to Torquay with a spare crew. It meant losing two days off, but there was a chance to earn extra wages, plus tips, so I agreed.

I was 17 and it was the first time I had worked with an all spare crew. On the selected day I arrived at Old Oak Common and boarded the train. If I remember right, we were due out of Paddington at about 11.30am and we were to do lunches and teas. I walked through the train and saw two cleaners coming towards me, both smiling and shaking their heads. On I walked, and when I reached the restaurant car I passed the kitchen and said to the chef, 'Cold for the time of year, chef!'

Back came the reply, 'Yes, darling. Cold enough for two hairnets.'

It was then I realised I was talking to Peter Gibson, known to everyone, except me, as 'The Queen Mother'. I was soon to find out that also on board was John Martin, known as 'Mary Martin', George Pegg, known as 'Peggy', and to finish off the conductor was called Bill Oakley, otherwise known as 'Annie Oakley'. Other than that everything was fine.

I think it would be safe to say that this particular trip was different. I was about to learn things I would never forget, such as how to put on mascara so that no one would realise it was being worn in the first place, together with all the things that could be done with colourless nail varnish. John, or was it Mary, told me that last night he could not find a colander, so had used his tennis racket as a strainer instead.

The actual trip went fine, and I was to realise that these four could work as hard as any of the regular lads. There was a slight scene when it was suggested that Peggy should help with the washing up. Something to do with nails. One of them did comment that all the steam coming from the kitchen would ruin one's hair-do and make it all go limp. They all thought it was outrageous when I called them 'my ansom'!

It was only when I was a little older that I was to learn that on some special trains, which were made up from spare staff, the dining car inspector was tipped to turn a blind eye to any faults. On these occasions it was a case of just walking in one door and out of the other. I think it was the handshake, given to the conductor on the platform, that gave the clue as to what was really taking place. That which is not seen cannot be reported.

A spare crew could pull many dodges. They could buy their own bread, cheese and ham to make up sandwiches and sell them for their own profit. This could also be done with their own tea, coffee and orange squash. All of these could be sold down the corridor to help turn a penny. Any ice-cream left over from lunch could be put into soufflé cases, and these could also go down the train. So as you can see, the crew would not want the inspector poking his nose in where it was not wanted. The really nasty scam was the swapping of wine labels. There was nothing easier than to steam the label off an expensive Macon or Medoc, and put it on to the cheapest plonk, which would have been bought from an off-licence.

It was only on these specials that such things took place. The 'Limited' would not have tolerated it. Not in a thousand

years. But even on the ' Limited' it was possible to do a little massaging of the system. When asked for a large Gordons gin, the BR measure was not used but a miniature Gordons opened instead. As these contained the equivalent of two and a half measures, the other half measure was put into the BR bottle, so enhancing the stock to our benefit.

It was usual when working the 'Duchy' up on a Friday for many American airmen to join us at Newbury, en route to London for the weekend. Lager was a new drink in England in those days, and we did sell it. The Americans always wanted lager and lime, so on a Friday morning we would try to obtain as much ice as we could in

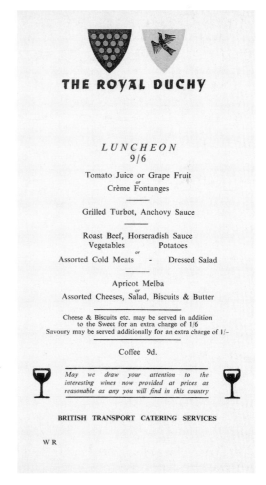

THE ROYAL DUCHY

LUNCHEON
9/6

Tomato Juice or Grape Fruit
or
Crème Fontanges

Grilled Turbot, Anchovy Sauce

Roast Beef, Horseradish Sauce
Vegetables   Potatoes
or
Assorted Cold Meats   -   Dressed Salad

Apricot Melba
or
Assorted Cheeses, Salad, Biscuits & Butter

Cheese & Biscuits etc. may be served in addition
to the Sweet for an extra charge of 1/6
Savoury may be served additionally for an extra charge of 1/-

Coffee 9d.

May we draw your attention to the interesting wines now provided at prices as reasonable as any you will find in this country

BRITISH TRANSPORT CATERING SERVICES

W R

Penzance and would pack it round bottles of light ale. When preparing a 'lager and lime' we would half fill two tumblers with ice, then add the chilled light ale and finally the lime. The sharp flavour of the lime would disguise the taste of the diluted light ale. The charge for this drink was 2s 9d; the light ale was 1s 6d, so we were on to a rather good thing. If ever it was suggested by an airman that it was not lager, we would get very indignant. We would point out that they were very lucky to get a drink at all, as this was a restaurant car and not a bar. We would tell them to show more gratitude. After all, we were doing them a favour.

There were many eccentric characters working on the dining cars in those days, and they were all hard-working. They also had an awesome reputation as hard drinkers, which was deserved by some. There are many good stories related to that activity. There was the night that one of the London 'Limited' lads bought a donkey in a Penzance pub, only to awake the next morning with no recollection of the previous evening's transaction. He was at first amused to see the farmer walk past the dining car with the donkey in tow as he was eating his breakfast. His mirth turned into horror when the previous night's activities were explained to him. I am sorry to say that I do not recall the outcome of this story.

However, I do recall a Polish chef who came here during the Second World War and stayed on at the end of hostilities. I cannot ever remember seeing him cold sober. His name was Jan, and he was another of the spare staff. He was very excitable, and it did not take much to push him over the top.

I was working with him on one occasion when he became very excited because he could not find the crimper for sealing the edge of a steak and kidney pie. After much shouting, first in English,

then in Polish, it all became too much for him. He gave up, took out the top set of his teeth, and used them instead. When the job was complete, he gave them a quick rinse and put them back into his mouth.

One day I was working spare and we were to take a late train out of Paddington to Plymouth, which only did dinners. When I boarded the train at Old Oak Common, mid-afternoon, I could tell that a disaster was about to happen. Jan came towards me with a half-empty bottle of Macon.

'Have a drink, my friend. Today is a very special day. It is the anniversary of the night when my best friend and I had to sleep in the snow during the war. It was so cold that my friend and I cuddled up to one another for warmth. But it was no good. In the morning, he was dead. I always take a drink today in his memory.'

As the afternoon wore on, it became obvious to us that Jan would be in no state to cook a chip, let alone a full dinner. One of the lads went up light to Paddington to inform our conductor of our little problem. Later, at the given time, our train was slowly pulled up to Paddington. By this time all Jan could do was to sit down and start singing in Polish. In fairness to the conductor, he was marvellous. He told one of us to take him down to the front of the train until we left Paddington. Our only worry was that a dining car inspector would decide to travel with us. The conductor was standing on number 1 platform giving out dinner tickets as if nothing was wrong.

At last we were on our way. As we passed Westbourne Park Jan was brought back to the diner. All we could serve that night was soup, fish, cheese and ice-cream. We had to explain to the passengers that the chef had been taken ill, and I am pleased to say that we were not very busy that evening. As for the passengers, I am sure they must have been curious as to who was singing in Polish from inside a locked toilet all the way down to Plymouth. This act was typical of the comradeship of those days. We looked after our own.

We also looked after others. It was 1956, the year that Premium Bonds were introduced, the year of the first Aldermaston march, and the start of the Suez Crisis, which the Anglo-French intervention failed to halt. Sir Anthony Eden was Prime Minister, but in the following year he retired, and Harold Macmillan became our leader, saying in July that '… most of our people have never had it so good.' In many ways I am sure he was right.

In those days, if a lad did anything wrong and was caught by the local Bobby he would receive a thick ear, then be escorted home and probably receive another from his father.

In those days you stood up for an old lady on a bus and were only too pleased to open a door for someone to go through. Perhaps I did go a bit far when I found a dead mouse in the gutter at Alverne Buildings. Thinking I was being helpful to a neighbour, I asked the lady of the house if she would like it for her cat, it not being too squashed and all. The ensuing scream brought her husband, who was having his tea in the kitchen at the back of the house, running the full distance through the hall to the front door. It seemed that she did not want it, and as the door was closing I heard him saying to her, 'I'm sure that boy is one chair short of a dining set.'

I was a bit put out by this. After all I was only trying to be helpful.

Also in 1956 Russia invaded Hungary. There was a great deal of sympathy for the refugees and, as usual in those days, Britain was trying to do her bit to help.

At that time I was working on the cars with other lads of my own age. There was

Johnny Watkins, who always had dark rings around his eyes and tended to look like a friendly panda, Tony Nicholls, and Ben Harvey, who worked on the 'Limited' with me. Ben's brother Edward also worked on the diners for a time, but later left us to become a skipper on one of the Newlyn trawlers.

I know we all thought that we would like to do something to help all those Hungarian refugees. The feeling was spontaneous, and out of this we created what was to become known as the Duchy Refugee Fund. We formed a committee, and John and I went to see Bill and Theo, the licencees of the Bath Inn in Cornwall Terrace, to see if we could have the use of their back room to hold committee meetings once a month. Being the nice folk that they were, they said yes.

The next thing to do was to get some cards printed, so I went to see a printer and told him that we wanted a card that folded in half, was about 4 inches long and 3½ inches wide, with 'Duchy Refugee Fund' printed on the front. On the inside there were to be thin horizontal lines with a line for the date down the side. After I had explained to him what they were for, he said he would print them at a reduced price for us. We paid for them from a collection we made amongst ourselves.

It was now that the fun started. Off we went to get staff to sponsor us on a regular basis – not much, two or three pence a week. If they agreed, they were given a card and each week it was marked off and entered into our master books that we carried with us. Rather like the man from the Pru…

We encouraged all the women who worked in the different refreshment rooms in the area we covered to chip in. It was great fun running into these places from the train to collect the weekly payments. Sometimes we cut it fine when the guard blew his whistle and we were still in the rooms, but somehow we managed.

Every month we had our meeting in the back room of the Bath Inn. The paperwork was soon completed, then the rest of the evening was left for us to sup a few brown ales. In due course the money was handed over to a representative of the town council to join the other money collected for that deserving cause.

6
LIFE AND DEATH

The day had started as normal. We had done all the work required of us at Old Oak Common, and we had even had a good breakfast. The run up from the Common had been uneventful, and the stores were waiting for us at platform 1. I had been over to the linen room to collect our order and for once it had been right. It looked by all accounts as though we were in for a good day. The the tickets for lunch were going steadily and we had more than enough ice to see us down to Cornwall. It was the Cornish crew who were on duty that day. I saw Bill, the guard, and he had the cleaning lady, Mary, with him. We had a full complement of staff.

It was a hot summer's day and the only slight irritation was that it might be a little too warm in the saloon when it came time to serve lunch. We did all the things we had done a thousand times before. There were the beers and wines to be checked and a chitty to be signed. As always, a dining car inspector boarded, walked up and down the saloon, and looked into the kitchen and the pantry to check that all was as it should be.

But it turned out that the day in question would be one to be remembered. The 'Limited' was to go from Paddington to Plymouth non-stop, with a slip coach for Westbury. We had done the two sittings of coffee, and were just preparing to do the calling in for first lunch when the guard came in all excited and in a fluster. He informed us that there was a woman who was about to give birth at any moment. He told us that Mary was with the woman and that they had managed to evacuate the other passengers from the compartment. He wanted to know if Jack Pascoe could help out, seeing that he had six children of his own. Jack was not very keen on the idea, and it was only after he had managed to down three bottles of Bass in quick succession that he would even consider the request. Shortly after this Mary appeared, and started to give both Jack and the guard some verbal abuse. She said to Jack, 'Come on, man. Anyone would think that you had no idea what to do.'

Her next remark sounded as if it had been taken from some cheap American B film. 'Come on, Michael. We need plenty of towels and some hot water.' Towels we could not supply, but we did have plenty of tablecloths.

Jack was looking sick, and requested another Bass, but Mary was having none of this, and started to push him out of the pantry. Both Jack and I took off our 'monkey jackets' and put our own jackets over our uniforms. At this stage there was a good deal of ribbing from the rest of the crew. The kitchen boy walked out of the kitchen with something stuffed up his apron. Another was on his knees doing his best to sing 'Baby Face'. As soon as we had our jackets on we were dipping into our pockets for cigarettes, and it was with a shaking hand that Jack offered me one.

Off we set, and we must have walked the length of two coaches before we came upon the ticket collector. 'Where the hell have you been? It'll be here at any moment!'

Mary was at the back with Jack in the middle, which left me facing the ticket collector. Mary gave Jack a push and he almost dropped the water. I did drop the tablecloths. We retrieved our composure and hurried to reach the compartment. All the blinds were down, and as Mary pushed open the door the sight before us confirmed the urgency of our mission.

I was told with short shrift by Mary to look the other way, and I was only too pleased to do so. The guard was now ejected, and I soon joined the concerned group outside the compartment. The guard was saying how pleased he was to see us, as he had no idea what to do. It did not take long and then there was a cry. Even in the corridor we could hear it. The woman had given birth to a boy. After what seemed an age to me, Jack's face emerged, the colour of a pillar box. He was out of breath.

'Son, go back to the car and bring two bottles of Bass and an opener.'

When I arrived back at the car and told the boys, there was a lot of clapping and cheering. The conductor said that Jack should be drinking champagne, and of course he could have another two Basses, and when it was sorted out Mary, the guard and the ticket collector must all come to the car to wet the baby's head. In the meantime could Jack and I get back as soon as possible, as there was work to do, and seeing that I had to go back down the train, could I do the calling in for the first lunch? Prior to getting the bottles for Jack I decided to have one myself. I did the calling in, and it was only on my way back that I was asked by a gentleman in the corridor what I meant by announcing, 'Seats for the first baby, please.'

We were stopped at Taunton and the woman was taken off to hospital.

A few weeks later the boss asked to have a word with Jack in his office. He was told that the parents of the baby had contacted the office and wanted to know if Jack would like to go to the christening. It seems that they were going to christen the baby Jack.

On the 'Limited' one day a little girl came into the car with her mother, father and younger sister, and she was crying. An eye had dropped out of her doll's head, had rolled along the compartment floor and could not be found. Her mother and father had brought her into the diner in the hope that being given a drink would in some way pacify her. But she was having none of it.

One of the two Jacks, who were on the crew, thought of an idea that might stop the tears. He bent down and made out that he was picking up a little dog, then he made out he was stroking it, and, after a little while, he handed it over to me.

'You can't hold him long, Mike – he'll be wanting his dinner.'

I made as if to put him down.

'I can't see no dog,' said the girl.

'I don't expect you can. He is only visible to little girls who don't cry,' replied Jack.

'What's his name?' she asked.

'Why, being Cornish his name is Kernow, of course,' I told her.

'I would love to see him,' she said, wiping the tears from her eyes. I had moved a short distance, and now I made as if to pick him up again. Jack said to her, 'Look, if you squint you'll be able to see him. Do you know that Mike and I are the only grown-ups to whom he is visible? Other than that he is only visible to good little girls who don't cry.'

She squinted. 'Yes! I can see him, I can see him!'

This really put the tin hat on it. Her sister started to cry. 'I want to see him mummy! I want to see him!'

Jack said, 'If you stop crying not only can you see him, but you can pick him up.

The crying stopped. I made as if to hand him over to her, and she began to stroke him. It was not long before the other one wanted him. So I took him off the little one, and gave him to the big one.

After a time Jack said to them both, 'This must be our secret. You mustn't tell anyone, or it'll break the magic.'

This was agreed upon.

Later, as I was doing the calling in, I looked down and found the missing eye. When I returned it the little girl asked me how I had found it, and I told her that it was not me, but Kernow, who had found it. She and her sister squealed with delight.

After this, if anything went wrong, the conductor would say, 'I expect it was that bloody dog.'

As you come over the Royal Albert Bridge at Saltash, if you look to your left you will see rows of houses, and among them are quite a few with conservatories. To people who do not know, they look like any other houses. But one of them was very special to us young lads on the 'Limited'. In one of these conservatories sat an old lady, and as we started to go over the bridge she would give us a wave. We would always stop what we were doing and wave back.

One day we were serving tea on the 'Limited' on the way to London, and were not very busy. I was taking teapots and putting them on the different tables and was not really taking much notice of what I was doing. As I put a teapot on one particular table a hand grabbed the sleeve

The approach to the Royal Albert Bridge at Saltash from the Cornish side in 1963. Some of the houses with their conservatories facing out across the Tamar can be clearly seen. *L. W. Ibbotson OBE, SLP collection*

of my jacket and pulled it. I looked down to see a small old lady with a hat on and a very wide smile. The first thing I thought was that when she was young she must have been very beautiful. With her sat a young man of about 25. On his face there was a smile also.

'Young man, you do not know who I am. Shame on you, after all this time.'

I took a longer look. She was wearing a flowery blouse topped by a light cream jacket. About her neck were two rows of beads, and on the table, next to her tea plate, there was a pair of cream gloves.

'Madam, you have the better of me,' I said.

'Then you are a very naughty boy, and there was me thinking that we were all friends. One can never tell.'

It was obvious to me that she was having great fun, so I kept it up.

'Now let me see,' I said. 'You are my grandmother, the one I have never met, and you have come to tell me that I have come into a fortune. This young man must be your solicitor.'

'No,' she replied. 'This young man with me is my grandson, and he is taking me to London for a treat. Such a nice boy. Not like some that I could mention.'

At this stage the young man was starting to look embarrassed.

'I think you had better tell him, gran. I don't think he is ever going to get it.'

Who should she be but the old lady who always waved to us from the conservatory.

'No wonder I couldn't tell. You're cheating. You've got a hat on,' I said. 'That's not fair.'

There was another smile and she said, 'You are not my only boyfriend. I have lots. I wave to them all as they go by.'

When the teas were finished and we had stripped off the tablecloths and put them into the linen bags, I sat down at their table for a nice long chat. I was going back to Old Oak Common that evening, so there was no rush. She told me that she had spent many years in South Africa living and working with her late husband. After he died she had returned to live with her son and daughter-in-law at Saltash. She told me many things in the time we had together and when we ran into Paddington she raised her hat to one side so that I could kiss her cheek.

After asking around a little, I found that indeed it was true. She did wave to all the boys. We were to see her in her usual place for about a further 18 months, then, one day, she was there no more...

Not all the incidents that occurred over the years were comic. Some were odd, some tragic. An example of the former was the time when I was working the 'Duchy' on an up trip and we had just left Newbury. A gent came into the dining car, sat down and ordered a fillet steak and all the trimmings. He had a dry sherry to start with, then a half bottle of Macon, and to end there was a large brandy and a black coffee. There was nothing unusual about this – he was a smart gent, well-spoken and carrying a briefcase, like thousands of others we served.

The conductor gave him some time before working out his bill. We were not busy that evening, and there were only two or three others in the car. When he was finally presented with the bill, we were in for a shock. He said to the conductor, 'I think that when we get to Reading you had better ring on to Paddington and get the Railway Police to meet us – you see, I have no money.'

We were all taken aback by this, and did just as he suggested when we got to Reading. When we reached Paddington the train was boarded by the police and the man arrested.

At that time the resident British Transport Police Officer at Penzance was Leonard Preece, who was also well-

G.W.R. HOTELS and CATERING SERVICES	£	s.	d.	
R. A. P. SETTERFIELD, Manager.				Station (7138)
BREAKFASTS				B
LUNCHEONS				L
DINNERS		5	4	D
GRILL				G
SOUP				S
FISH				F
ENTREE				E
JOINT				J
VEGETABLES				V
SWEETS				S
SAVOURIES				S
Bread				B
Butter				B
Cheese				C
Salad				S
Cream				C
Sundries				S
Tea,Coffee,Cocoa,&c.				T
ALE or STOUT		2		A
WINES				W
SPIRITS				S
LIQUEURS				L
MINERAL WATERS				M
CIGARS				C
	£			
No. of Persons	TABLE No	WAITER		
	D	13984		

trained in first aid. He lived at Gulval, and was later to move to Southampton Docks. I always found him to be a kind person, yet well aware of his responsibilities.

As far as I can remember I only worked the 'Cornishman' once. This train ran daily between Penzance and Wolverhampton, and the crew, like those on the 'Limited', would find themselves in digs for the night at Wolverhampton, returning to Penzance the following day. We were serving lunch on the down trip, and occupying the window seats at a table for four were a man and his wife. We had just served soup to the man and placed a grapefruit in front of his wife. Moments

Left A GWR restaurant car bill. Usually customers had the means of payment! *Author's collection*

Below I only worked the 'Cornishman' once. Running between Wolverhampton and Torquay/Penzance, the northbound train is seen here at Burlescombe on the climb to Whiteball Tunnel between Tiverton Junction and Taunton. *Lens of Sutton*

later as I walked past I saw that the man had slumped forward with his head resting in his soup. As you can imagine, the lady was in a state; she called me over, and I in turn fetched the conductor, who very soon was able to to confirm that the man was dead.

The poor woman – I shall never forget the look on her face. It took some time for the information to sink in, and when it did there was no consoling her. I was sent off to get the guard, and at the next station the train was held while a doctor was called to pronounce the poor man dead. After a considerable time his body was removed and we were able to go on our way.

I recall another time when I was working the 'Duchy' on a down trip. We had left Plymouth and I was calling in a sitting of light refreshments. I slid open one compartment door and made my announcement. The compartment contained a woman on her own, and I could see from the look on her face that there was something not quite right. I waited a few moments then inquired if she was all right. In return she gave me a very strange look, turning her head as if in slow motion, but said nothing. I had to get on, so off I went.

However, I had not gone very far when the train entered a tunnel. All of a sudden there was a loud screeching noise, and for a moment I thought that we were going to come off the tracks. Someone had pulled the communication cord. On investigation we found that the woman had thrown herself from the compartment and been killed. We were to spent some time there while the police were contacted, and the next day at Penzance I had to give a full statement to the railway police.

One day I was working the up trip on the 'Duchy', and when we pulled in at Exeter St Davids the station master boarded the train. This was not a usual occurrence, and should have given us a warning that something was amiss. He asked if he could talk to the kitchen boy. He stepped forward, rather nervously – he was only 16 – and the station master said to him, 'I am sorry to put it to you like this lad, but I can't hold the train. Your mother had a heart attack after you left for work this morning, and I am sorry to have to tell you that she has since died. Now lad, what would you like to do? Get off here and go home on the next down train, go on to Paddington and catch a later train back, or perhaps even work your own train back with your mates tomorrow? But you must tell me now, as I must let the train go.'

The look of pain on the boy' s face was something I would not wish to see again.

'Come on, lad. You must tell me.'

The boy said that he would stay on the train and complete the trip. The whistle was blown and off we went. As you might imagine, the crew were embarrassed, as only the British can be about death. Moreover, the suddenness of the event managed to intensify the desolate atmosphere. We busied ourselves and tried to keep out of the kitchen boy's way.

The day wore on, and it was time to serve teas. I went to the kitchen hatch and shouted, 'Right away the tea cakes!'

It was the lad who gave them to me on a silver salver. I looked at his face and the tears were still pouring down his cheeks and on to the top of his apron.

He then went missing for some time. He had locked himself in the toilet so that he could do his grieving alone. We left him there until Paddington, but even then he did not want to come out.

We all went back to Old Oak Common, where we sat eating our supper. He rushed to the toilet again and locked himself in. The conductor left him there for some time, but when it was time to leave the train, he knocked on the door.

'Come on, lad, don't fret so. Your ma wouldn't like to see you going on like this.'

A short time later he came out. We all walked out of the shed together and went to the nearest pub, taking the boy with us. We all had pints, including the lad. One of the staff gave him a cigarette, but he started to cough, and when he lifted his pint he managed to spill it down his chest. This could not go on, obviously.

'Look my ansom,' said the conductor, 'why don't you go back home tonight? You could be home with your dad in the morning.'

He gave it some thought and decided that it would be best. The conductor asked me if I would travel light with him back to Paddington, and see him off. This I agreed to do. I stayed with him until it was time for his train to go, and as the whistle went to signal the departure he looked at me with a tear-stained face, and was gone.

One of the saddest days of all my time on the railways was the day that a lad called Brian Veal was killed. It appears that he slipped between the gangways, and that was that. What a shock it must have been for Billy Matthews, the Penzance driver that day, who was working an 0-6-0 pannier tank. Brian was just 20 years of age. Even after all these years I think back to that dreadful day with great sadness. The strange thing about it was that he should not have been there in the first place; he had swapped shifts that day.

7
MUCK AND GOLD

So far it had been a good day, and we had been very busy, with two full sittings for lunch. After this we took a short break for our own meal, then served tea. With all of this going on a good bit of rubbish accumulated during the course of a day. In the pantry, under the window, there was a large rubbish bin into which all the rubbish was deposited, quite often to overflowing. To try to help the situation, I asked the kitchen staff if I could put some of mine in their bin. I think that one can imagine their reply to this request. So in desperation I used a tin bowl on the side, directly above the large rubbish bin. When this also became full, I felt that there was no alternative but to grab the leather window strap, lower the window and throw the rubbish out.

Over the years I must have done this many hundreds of times with no comebacks, but all good things must come to an end. This was to be my day of reckoning. When we ran into Paddington, a dining car inspector met the train. He came to me and said, 'Son, did you throw any muck out of the window on the way up?'

All at once I could feel myself becoming hot, and in a few seconds my heart was in my mouth. Lew Gordon was not a man to be messed with. Of all the inspectors, he was the one most feared by the youngsters on the crew, even when nothing was wrong. One glance from Lew Gordon and everyone began to feel guilty,

rather like one does when going through the green aisle of a customs post at an airport, even with nothing to declare. This time, however, I felt sure I detected a slight grin on his face. Surely not – in all the time I had known him, I had never seen him smile. But there it was again. I must be going mad, I thought.

'I think that you'd better come over to the office with me, lad. The boss wants a word with you.'

My legs felt like jelly. To be called to head office to see the boss in the company of Mr Gordon – this had to be the end.

As we walked from platform 8, passing all the other platforms and the shops, then down platform 1, past the big clock and and number 1 refreshment rooms, we did not speak. In number 1 bay was the 'Cheltenham Spa Express', and as we approached Mr Gordon put his hand out for me to stop. 'You just wait there, my lad.'

Off he went and started talking to the conductor and an attendant off the 'Spa', who were giving out meal tickets. After a few seconds, all three turned to look at me. Then, horror upon horror, they all started to laugh, even the demented inspector. After another few seconds, the chef's head was out of the window, and the attendant was whispering into his ear, then he too was taken with a fit of laughter. They must all be taking leave of their senses. I could see nothing funny in the slightest.

The concourse at Paddington was known as 'The Lawn', and is seen here in April 1960. It was across here that I was marched by dining car inspector Lew Gordon to face the boss. *L. W. Ibbotson OBE, SLP collection*

After what seemed an age, Mr Gordon waved for me to follow him. In we went. As this was the head office for the whole of the dining cars on the Western Region, it was always a busy place. In total unison, the whole of the office came to a stop. There were at least nine girls typing when we entered. Now one could hear a pin drop. I was marched past all the girls and came to a stop in front of Mr Groves, the number one man. Looking over his shoulder, at the door through which we had just entered, I could see my Doris from the linen room, her huge body taking up the whole of the doorway. She raised her hand in a gesture of reassurance. I gave a nod in return.

I stood rigid in front of Mr Groves's desk, rather like that famous painting 'When did you last see your Father?'. After what seemed ages, he said, 'Now

young man, did it you throw some shit out of the window on the way up today?

'No sir,' I lied.

Lew Gordon lent over the desk and whispered something into his ear. Mr Groves sat up straight and said, 'Mr Gordon here tells me that there is a large streak down the side of the coach, which could only have been put there by such an action. What have you to say to that?'

My heart was pounding so hard in my chest that I thought at any moment it would stop.

'Nothing sir,' I replied.

'Well, my boy! I have a great deal to say to you, and the first thing is this. You would not have known, but when you did throw it out of the window you were going through Taunton, and unfortunately for you it just so happens that today the station master had a delegation of French railway officials he was escorting, and they caught the lot.'

The silence was almost unbearable. I could just imagine the station master with his top hat on, and I thought that my world was about to end. In the reflection in the glass of a picture on the wall I could see that all the women were having a good laugh. As far as I could see the only one not laughing was my Doris, who was still standing in the doorway.

'I have to tell you this. We cannot put up with this kind of behaviour. Not only are you letting the side down, but it is downright dangerous.'

Even I could see that what he was saying was true. We had the famous *King George V* up front, and we frequently went through Taunton at a tremendous rate.

'I suspend you from duty for three days, and let that be a lesson to you. Do you hear?'

It was as if someone had hit an action button. Everything was back to normal. The girls took up their typing again, and I soon found myself on the way out of the office, only to be caught by Doris, who managed to push my head between her ample breats yet again. She started to stroke my hair.

'My poor love! I thought that you'd had it that time.'

Although I was grateful for her concern, I was now in great danger of suffocation. Surely I had had enough excitement for one day!

The 'Cheltenham Spa Express' was always a prestigious train. It ran from Cheltenham to Paddington, going from Kemble to London non-stop; in the morning breakfasts and coffees were served, and teas and dinners on the return trip. One day I was talking to Cyril Cowley, who was the conductor on this train for many years. He told me that he had served two or three generations of the same family on this run. Indeed, one day

when I was working the 'Spa', a lady came up to Cyril at Paddington and handed into his care two children, a boy of about ten, and his sister, who would have been about eight. They had dinner and, when asked if they would like sweet or cheese, they chose the latter. I do not know why I should remember this detail, but perhaps

I turned 21 in 1959, this photo marking the occasion.

it was the serious expression on their faces when they made their choice. I remember thinking that they were very 'county'. Cyril assured me that he had seen many such children over the years. They were met at Kemble by their father and Cyril was handed a tip for his trouble.

Back in 1960 the 'Cheltenham Spa Express' left Cheltenham St James's at 7.55am and arrived into Paddington at 10.35am. Breakfasts started on leaving Gloucester at 8.19am. There was a choice of porridge, cornflakes, Weetabix or fruit juices, orange, grapefruit or tomato. This was followed by either a fish course or a main course. The fish would be either kippers, haddock or even plaice or brill, the latter from the previous evening's dinner menu. The main course consisted of bacon and egg, sausage and bacon or sausage and tomato, all served with sauté potatoes and grilled tomatoes. Toast and tea or coffee followed.

Ideally, by the time the train was approaching Stroud the main course had been served. At that time there were 42

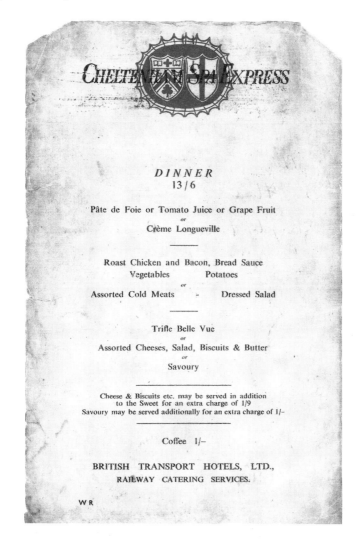

CHELTENHAM SPA EXPRESS

DINNER
13/6

Pâte de Foie or Tomato Juice or Grape Fruit
or
Crème Longueville

Roast Chicken and Bacon, Bread Sauce
Vegetables   Potatoes
or
Assorted Cold Meats   -   Dressed Salad

Trifle Belle Vue
or
Assorted Cheeses, Salad, Biscuits & Butter
or
Savoury

Cheese & Biscuits etc. may be served in addition
to the Sweet for an extra charge of 1/9
Savoury may be served additionally for an extra charge of 1/-

Coffee 1/-

BRITISH TRANSPORT HOTELS, LTD.,
RAILWAY CATERING SERVICES.

W R

seats in the restaurant car, and if everything went to schedule the second sitting for breakfast started just after Swindon. If a busy exhibition, like the Boat Show or the Motor Show, was in progress, there might even be a third sitting, then usually one or two sittings of coffee. There were six crew members; one of them, David Staite, the kitchen boy, became my friend and still is.

Many Cheltenham businessmen went by car to Kemble and caught the train from there. It took an hour for the train to get from Cheltenham to Kemble because of the time it took for the train to climb through the Stroud valley, but it was only half an hour's run by car.

On the down trip the train used to leave Paddington at 4.55pm, and the timing allowed two sittings of afternoon tea and one sitting of dinner. The train would finish its run at 7.35pm, making it a long day for the staff. Afternoon tea would consist of either a toasted teacake or toast, sandwiches, usually tomato or egg, and bread and butter, brown or white. To finish the choice was either a slice of cake or a pastry. All of this for 3s 6d.

It must be remembered that we used to cook everything on the trains, except for the bread and ham. Many a time I can recall seeing the chef cutting through a chine bone of beef. His soup stock pot was always on the stove. At that time, all the restaurant cars used oil gas, but went on to use propane when the Series 1905 dining cars came into service.

When Sir Brian Robertson was Chairman of British Railways, he used this train to journey to London on a Monday morning, and many a time the train arrived a good 5 minutes early. As the 'Cheltenham Spa Express' arrived, the 'Cornish Riviera Express' was leaving platform 1, at 10.30am. When as a pantry boy working the 'Riviera' up to Paddington, I was once asked by an

inspector to work the 'Cheltenham Spa Express' down to Cheltenham the same evening, sleep in a First Class compartment in St James's sidings, then work the train up in the morning. Because the 'Spa' arrived at 10.35am and the 'Riviera' left at 10.30am, I would miss it, so the inspector took the pantry boy off the 'Duchy' to work the 'Riviera', and I worked the 'Duchy' to Penzance. This meant two 12-hour working days, which would not be allowed now, but I do not think it did me any harm.

I liked to work the 'Spa'. There was always a good atmosphere, rather like an Old Boys' Club. All the regular travellers used to call the staff by their first names, and some of them were so well known that they did not have to ask for an aperitif; it was put down in front of them as they sat down. This was truly a great train.

I only worked one boat train, and on reflection it must have been one of the last from Plymouth. I believe the old GWR Jubilee rolling-stock was used. The train was made up of saloons, which were split up to make then look like rooms. The settees, with plush upholstery, and the individual seats were large and comfortable. The windows were draped in velvet, and brass was very much in evidence, giving the impression of a life of luxury with no expense spared. I could just imagine an Edwardian gentleman, with his extremely elegant wife, sitting there, he smoking a cigar, she doing her intricate needlework, and sitting beside them two gorgeous children with Pears complexions. To complete the picture there would be a golden labrador at his master's feet!

In reality, I found myself in the pantry, making up mustard. I and the rest of the crew had already been on the train for some time, and when I happened to look into the first saloon I saw one of the smartest-dressed men I have ever seen. He wore striped morning trousers, shoes so

I only worked on one boat train. This restaurant car on a French Line 'Ocean Special' from Plymouth was photographed at Newton Abbot in 1959. *L. W. Ibbotson, SLP collection*

clean that they shone like glass, and a light grey overcoat, which had black velvet lapels on it. He was carrying a rolled edition of the *Daily Telegraph* and was holding a silver-topped cane. On his head he sported a very stylish trilby.

Thinking that one of the passengers had managed to get on the train early, I approached him and said, 'Sorry, sir, but we are far from ready to supply any food. If you would like to return to your seat, someone will call you when we are ready.'

He stared at me for some moments, then said, 'Not to worry, old boy. I am not a passenger – I am your conductor for the day.'

He then began to peel off his doeskin gloves. 'Now be a good chap and get me a glass of tea, please.' Then, unfolding the *Telegraph*, he spread it on the table. 'I can tell you this, old thing. There is much research work to do here.'

Off I went to get the tea. I could not stop smiling, as I had never met a person like this before. I returned to the table with the tea. He just waved his arm, indicating for me to set it down. He seemed to be mumbling something about the Queen Mother and the Duchess of Kent. Then, with a gold pencil, he began to make rings around entries in the newspaper's Court Circular.

After some time he came to the pantry. 'Say, dear boy. Do you think that you could knock me up a pink gin? Not too much angostura and no ice.'

He then went off to change. On his return, he asked the chef if he could have some melba toast. When the toast was ready, I took it to him, together with the pink gin. Prior to my arrival, he had managed to produce some Gentleman's Relish. As he took the toast from me, I noticed that his fingers were long and that there was a gold ring on the little finger of his right hand.

I carried on with my work. When most of the chores were done, I returned to the saloon to clear the table, and while doing so I noticed that the *Telegraph* was the previous day's edition.

Then we were off. The passengers, most of them American, were trying to find their reserved seats in the different saloons. The conductor came to me and said, 'Now, young man, you are to be my personal assistant for the day. Stick close to me and you could learn a lot – and don't speak unless you are spoken to.'

The first job was to offer the passengers an aperitif. In the first saloon we entered there was as an American with his wife and children. He was dressed in a heavy check jacket, and around his neck hung a disc with a small picture on it attached to what looked like a pair of shoelaces. The man was fat, as was his wife, who was dressed in a lilac tracksuit. Around her neck she wore half the gold that should have been in Fort Knox. White stilettos covered her feet, and her nails were painted scarlet. By the look of it she had had a facelift that had gone slightly wrong. Their three children were a reflection of their parents. The boy was plump and gave the impression that if he was pricked with a pin he would explode. The two girls were about 13 and 16. The elder had a brace on her teeth, and small round brass-rimmed glasses on her nose. Her younger sister had her hair parted in the middle with plaits hanging either side of her head. The girls were dressed in gingham dresses, one blue, the other red. The boy, who was about 12, was dressed in check jeans and was also sporting a check shirt. The impression they gave was something like watching a car crash in slow motion.

The elegant conductor took one look and said 'Good God' out of the side of his mouth. After a short pause we entered the saloon.

'Good day to you all and welcome to England. My boy and I hope that you will have a pleasant stay in our country,' said the conductor.

There was a few moments silence, then the woman said, or rather sang, to her husband, 'Gee, Homer, what a nice thing to say to us.'

Homer nodded, but said nothing at this point. The two girls started to giggle, and even the boy stopped picking his nose for a second.

Then Homer said, 'Say, fella, is it possible to get a drink around here?'

'Indeed it is, sir. That is why my boy and I are here. What would you like?'

After some thought Homer said he would like a genuine Scotch whisky, the wife wanted a Screwdriver, and the three children lemonades. Homer said they would like lots of ice. The conductor said that he could have a whole iceberg if he wished. At this point the wife sneezed.

'Goodness gracious me, madam, I hope that you have not caught a chill. Why, it was only yesterday that the same thing happened when we had the pleasure to attend Her Majesty Queen Elizabeth, The Queen Mother.'

All at once there were five mouths hanging open at the same time. Homer shifted in his seat, then said, 'Yesterday? The Queen Mother?'

A smile came over my colleague's face. 'Yes, indeed, sir. We were most concerned about her.'

This was too much for Homer. He shook his head. 'Now let's get this right, fella. Are you telling me that yesterday you were attending the Queen Mother here in this very carriage?'

'Nothing strange about that, sir,' the conductor replied. 'We do it quite often.' Then, looking at me for confirmation, said, 'Don't we, Perkins?'

I replied that this was indeed the case, thinking that this man should be on the stage… He then went on to say, 'You see, we took Her Majesty from London to Bath in this very saloon.'

The American wife was now shaking from head to toe in excitement.

'You just wait, Homer! As soon as I get back I'll ring the Schwalzes and tell them this. Just think what we had to put up with when they had an audience with the Pope in Rome last year, and there were three thousand others with them, and here we are in the Queen Mother's dining saloon! We must take photos – would you take some photos for us?'

The conductor said, 'First things first. There will be plenty of time to take photos later. Really, madam, we must get on and get your drinks.' To Homer he said, 'There is just one thing, sir. It is a tradition that whoever travels in the Royal Saloon buys the staff a drink.'

Homer waved his hand. 'Anything you want, fella.'

To this my colleague said, 'Twenty gin and tonics, Perkins. Put them on your list.'

I was gone in a flash. I did indeed learn a lot that day.

Later on an attendant rushed up to the conductor and told him that we were running short of coffee.

'No need to worry,' he was told. 'Just put some gravy browning in with it. It will do nothing to the taste but it would help it go a lot further.'

When later, back on my own train, I told the lads about my experiences on the boat train, one of them told me that the conductor on that trip was a former head steward off the liners, and that he had quite a reputation. This I could well believe.

On the subject of 'Royalty', at the time of the nationalisation of the railways in 1948 it was decided that a certain few directors of the former private railway companies should be given a 'Gold Pass',

which would allow them to travel free on any part of the system. When encountering such personages it was in one's own interest to treat them as if they were Royalty. These people had no official clout, but it would be a very foolish person who thought that their influence was not sought and acted upon. It was to be like this for many years.

Often we would go to the notice board in the passage next to the office, and there would be a message for the crew that read 'Special Attention Please' followed by a short message such as 'Today you will have travelling with you The Hon Barrington-Smythe, son of Lord Hunter of Trewithan. The Hon, it must be noted, likes plenty of ice with his drinks. The Hon does not like English mustard. Please ensure that you have on board a supply of French mustard. The Hon smokes Players Tipped. Please make sure these are in plentiful supply. He will alight at Bodmin Road. Make sure he has assistance in alighting from the train.'

Receiving such a message as this, we made sure that a 'Reserved' notice was put on a table for two in the First Class saloon. We also made sure that no one would sit with our guest on the vacant seat opposite, unless invited to do so by the 'Special Attention Please' person. I remember once, when we had travelling with us the actor Sir Michael Redgrave, that a woman passenger was quite upset because I would not let her sit with him.

There was one complaint from a 'Special Attention Please' passenger. It seems that an attendant had asked a lady if she would like stuffing with her roast pork, while pointing the ladle in the direction of her plate. There followed a message posted to all crews on the notice board, reading: 'To all Personnel. It is absolutely imperative that under no circumstances do you ask female passengers if they would like stuffing. In future you must say "Madam, do you require seasoning?" If this directive is not acted upon, it could lead to extreme disciplinary action being taken against you. All staff must sign the enclosed copy, and it should be returned to the office as soon as possible.' I am assured that Madam was a Gold Pass carrier.

Looking back now to the 1950s, it seems a world away from today. If all those Gold Pass carriers could see what we accept now as normal, they would think they were on another planet.

We had one 'Special Attention Please' notice informing us that there would be a gentleman travelling with his wife and nurse, going down as far as Plymouth. Unfortunately the poor man had had a stroke and could hardly move. We were informed that their meals were to be served in their compartment, which was First Class next to the restaurant car.

Shortly after we set off the nurse said that madam would like to talk to one of us. Madam felt that her husband was trying to indicate that he wished to make a bowel movement. She realised that it was not usually done, but did we think we could take him to the toilet. She assured us that we would be rewarded with a tip for carrying out such a task. It was down to Jerry Sergeant and me to do the necessary. The man was a dead weight and it took all our strength to get him inside the lavatory. When we had succeeded, we had to decide who was going to undo the poor man's trousers. He was making a great deal of noise, grunting to such a degree that I thought he was about to do something most unpleasant. Needless to say, it was down to me to do the honours with the trousers. After some considerable manoeuvring, me managed to settle him on the seat. By now we could both see the comic situation we were in, and it was only by not looking at each other that we could avoid laughing out loud.

Lavatories on board were pretty basic. It was in one like this that Jerry Sergeant and I struggled to assist a disabled passenger. *David Harvey*

Then it started. I had never heard such a noise in my life. The poor man was straining to such a degree that I thought he was about to explode. We managed to lift him, but nothing had happened. We sat him back down for a complete repeat performance. After a short while I noticed he was turning an alarming shade of purple. I made a sign to breathe out, as I thought that he had been trying to hold his breath. Thank goodness, at that moment a knock came at the door and the nurse was calling to see if we were all right. I managed to open the door a fraction and informed her that our charge was changing colour like a chameleon on heat. She gave a small cry. It seemed he was having one of his turns.

'Take out one of these small pills and put it under his tongue.'

She managed to put her hand through a gap in the door. All I could see was the starched cuff of her uniform. The small pills were the same colour as our charge, in a small black and white bottle, which had some handwriting in black. They had been dispensed in Harley Street.

It was a few minutes before the pills took effect, and he started to return to a normal colour. Jerry had taken to a silent fit of laughter at the whole situation and had his hankie in his mouth. He had slid open the small top window to obtain some air, and was doing all within his power not to look at me. The man's wife was now at the door.

'Darling, please try your hardest for me. Take your time, dear. There is no hurry, no hurry at all.'

It was then that both Jerry and I decided that enough was enough. We gave it a few more minutes, then started to get him dressed again.

Now there was another knock at the door. It was the conductor. What the hell did we think we were up to? He had a full sitting in the car and was short of two hands.

As we eased the gent back into his seat his wife asked, 'Did he manage anything?'

When we informed her that he had not, she was most upset. 'Now really, darling, after all my hard work, you have let me down.'

As we were about to leave, she put a 10 shilling note in my hand.

After we had had our own meal, the nurse came and asked if we could do it all again for madam, or for sir, to be more precise, and we did. Now that is what I call service. Would such a thing happen today? Really the poor man should not have been travelling in the first place.

One Gold Pass holder who used to travel with us on a regular basis was Lord Morley. He was the very epitome of one's preconceived idea of what a Lord should look like. He was always very well turned out, with a smart suit, usually a thin classic stripe, and a white shirt with a small amount of cuff showing at the bottom of the sleeve of the jacket. Thin gold cufflinks were always in evidence and, if my memory serves me right, a Brigade of Guards tie. His black shoes always had a shine that would compare favourably with new shoes in a shop window. He had thin swept-back hair with a slight parting on the right-hand side. He was not very tall, but walked with an assurance that advertised his place in society.

He would always travel on a Friday from Plymouth to Paddington. He was not a true 'Special Attention Please' person, just a regular passenger. I think I am right in saying that the tunnel not far from Plymouth, going north, is called Morley Tunnel after his family name.

When the 'Riviera' was at Plymouth on the up trip, the conductor and at least one attendant would be on the platform giving out lunch tickets. Not that his Lordship would require one, as the first table for two, next to the car, was always reserved for him on Fridays. He would walk up to our staff on the platform and say, 'Good day.'

Their response would be a slight bow and, 'Good day, my Lord.'

This would be said in unison, then there would be a clicking of heels that would put even the SS to shame. Once he had taken his seat in the restaurant car, Lord Morley would stay there for the whole trip. When the ticket collector and guard passed through the restaurant car and spotted his Lordship, they would stop in front of him and give a slight bow. His Lordship never had any luggage with him, only the *Financial Times*.

There was a set routine when waiting on his Lordship. He would always have a large pink gin, Gordons, and with it a tipped cigarette. Both would be presented to him on a silver salver. The cutlery that was set before him was always washed separately in soapy water, as was the glass tumbler. A starched napkin, spotlessly clean, was also required. The vase, containing fresh flowers, was also given a good wash and filled with clean water. If the flowers were drooping for some reason they would not be put out. As soon as we left the station a plate of melba toast and a saucer of butter pats were served together with crushed ice sprinkled on the top and garnished with fresh parsley.

There was one occasion, however, when things did not work quite like clockwork. During the summer it was not unusual to have some of the lads off the liners working spare with us; quite often they would take the summer off so that they could have some time with their families, and to keep up their income they would work for BR for the season, returning to sea for the winter.

One of them was an Irish lad called Pat. In fact, he was to work with us quite often under this arrangement. On this particular day I was dispensing the drinks. There was a certain way of doing this, which I will explain in a moment. Anyway, I made up his Lordship's drink, and when it was ready I said to Pat, 'Give this to first left back this way – also give him a cigarette and present both drink and cigarette on a silver salver.'

I carried on doing the drink orders and after a few moments Pat said, 'Mike, have you any fags?'

I replied that I had not, and carried on. Nothing more was said. It was only when I was walking through the saloon that I caught sight of Pat serving his Lordship. It was too late for me to do anything, but I could not believe my eyes. There on the salver was a 'roll-up', so thin that it consisted mostly of paper. His Lordship picked up his drink, then the roll-up, and

said to Pat, 'What the deuce is this, old man?'

Pat replied, 'You'll be enjoying that. It's my best Golden Virginia, so it is.'

With this, out came the lighter. I shall always remember his Lordship's huffing and puffing. Quickly I rushed back to the pantry, opened a new pack of Players Tipped, and went to the rescue. No real harm was done, but we kept Pat well away from Lord Morley in future.

When the journey ended at Paddington, his Lordship would always walk up to the driver and the fireman, shake their hands and give them a tip. It was not unknown for him to stroke the engine, if it were on time, rather like stroking a pet.

Often one attendant would go about the saloon taking drink orders, while another dispensed them, with yet another actually taking the drinks to the passenger. The system we used was that if you looked up the saloon, you would have tables on your left and on your right. In First Class the tables for two were on the left and for four on the right. So if someone was sitting on the third table on the right next to the aisle facing us, that person would be 'third right outside facing'. If he was sitting at the fifth table for two on the left-hand side with his back to us, he would be 'fifth left back this way' and so on. It worked well.

On one occasion when I was calling in on the 'Limited' I saw two monks and an old lady approaching me. I made room for them to pass, and the three of them went into the restaurant car. The two monks were dressed in brown habits secured around the waist by a white rope, which had three knots tied in it. On their feet they had sandals, but no socks. I found them both very pleasant; they had a beer each with their meal and when they were given the bill it was the lady who paid. On the trains you would meet all sorts of people so I thought nothing more about them.

When my mother came home from the Queens Hotel that evening she told me that there were two monks and an old lady staying there. The next day was my day off and in the evening I was walking along the Promenade and who should I see coming towards me but the younger of the two monks. He stopped and asked me if it was my mother who was looking after them at the hotel; the chambermaid had told her that one of her sons worked on the trains. We stood for some time talking and I suggested that we should return home for a coffee and a chat.

I learned that the two monks were in fact Franciscan friars. Father Donald, the younger one, was being treated by his mother to a small holiday in the company of Father David before going to New Guinea to work as a missionary. We must have chatted for two or three hours, and I found him very interesting company. Apparently prior to becoming a friar he had been in the Royal Navy for some years. From what he told me he had had a very interesting life. He even invited me to go and stay at The Mother House in Dorset, but I declined.

If I had known then what was to be the outcome of that meeting I would not have believed it in a million years, for when I left the railway in 1964 I became a Franciscan novice; but that is another story.

Over the years I was to meet a good many celebrities. At the height of his success we took Bill Haley and his Comets from Paddington to Plymouth on the 'Limited'. They were quite a friendly crowd, but a noisy one. Bill was giving press interviews in his compartment. The whole party had tickets for the second lunch, but it was a deuce of a job to get them to take their seats. They all wanted to wonder in in dribs and drabs, but this would not do at all.

We started a full sitting about half an hour late and it put us back for the rest of the day. When that kind of thing happened it would upset the chef, and don't let anyone tell you that chefs are not temperamental, because they are. If they were ever caught out having not prepared for the number of lunches booked, they would put the soup plates in the oven and put the gas full on. When the time came to start the sitting, the plates would be so hot that they could not be handled. This would delay the start of the meal for some time, and give the chef a chance to catch up.

Tommy Steele had a hit with 'Singing the Blues' in 1956. When we had him on the 'Limited' he was very friendly. He visited the kitchen, had a chat with the staff and left a handsome tip. I think he knew how hard we worked, but then he would, as he had worked on the liners prior to reaching fame.

Alma Cogan, bless her, was charming. It was so sad that she was to die so very young. Eve Boswell was also charming.

I could fall into the trap here of listing dozens of celebrities whom I met over the years, but I won't. I was, however, very pleased to meet Richard Sharp, the Cornish rugby player. He was a great hero at the time.

One thing for which I will always be grateful was living and working in London at the time when it was just possible to see live variety prior to its execution by television. When on the 'Limited' I was able to go to the London Palladium on very many occasions. One day Les Pender and I went to see Danny Kaye there, and Les made a noise like a chicken just for a laugh. Danny took this up and went into an elaborate dance routine as if he were a chicken. This is Les's claim to fame. Later in the show a man in the stalls called out that Danny was rubbish. Whether he was a plant or not I do not know, but Danny called for the house lights to be put up, and he and this man had a right slanging match. When it was over the man walked out.

Another theatre that we used to frequent was the Empire at Shepherds Bush, which went on to become the BBC Television Theatre. At about this time there was a show called 'Thanks For The Memory', and I went to see it at the Met in Edgware Road. I was spellbound. I saw G. H. Elliott, Hettie King and Dougie Bing, as well as many others I cannot now recall. What memories!

The railways have always had a strong tie with variety. At the heyday of live theatre it was nothing to see many of them at Crewe station on a Sunday, all charging off to another town for another week's work. Many hours were spent at this station, giving them a chance to discuss digs with each other. I am informed that it was nothing unusual to see trick cyclists practising on the platforms. It has also been said that it was at Crewe that a comic was looking at the words 'No Smoking' on a carriage window, moved the letters around and went on to have a very successful career as Nosmo King. Thank goodness I was just in time to see it all.

8
EPILOGUE: OUT OF STEAM

The former Great Western Railway engine No 6000 *King George V*, mentioned earlier, is I suspect one of the most famous railway engines not only in this country but also in the world. If when in conversation with steam enthusiasts I happen to mention that I worked on the railway at the time I did, they will often talk about this locomotive in the same way that one might talk about an adoring mistress. I myself have never been smitten like this about any engine. True, I can appreciate the incredible precision engineering that went into the manufacture of these machines, and indeed there is nothing like the sight of one of these engines going at top speed. Having been lucky enough to have seen *King George V* in full cry, it is not something that I am likely to forget.

The devotion that some of the old engine drivers and firemen gave to these beasts is almost beyond description. They would go to almost impossible lengths to make sure that their charges were performing to capacity output. What better memories could one have than seeing a driver, in his overalls, cravat and cap, leaning out of his cab with soot on his face? Or to see a fireman with his shovel feeding the coal into the firebox with all the effort that he could muster? These men were craftsmen. Just by listening they knew if their maiden was in a mood to do them proud, or if she was having an off

day. I always found it amusing that they would talk about them as feminine – she did this or she would not do that.

They would say things like, 'She was not up to it today.' Or, 'If I had given her her head, she would have taken off like a flying carpet.' When it came time for these men to retire they would say, 'No one can handle her like me', or, 'She has to be treated with a kindly hand. She can't abide being bullied.' Then off they would go to their real wives.

It was not unusual to see these men, shortly after their retirement, hanging about the station. The only reason they did this was for a chance to see their mistresses again. But of course they would not admit it. They would say things like, 'Just thought I'd get a breath of fresh air', or, 'I came down to get the new timetable.' They knew and we knew why they were there, yet to them it would somehow seem unmanly to admit it.

When on occasions I had to walk out to the Long Rock depot at Penzance, I would see all sorts of wonders. I would never have thought that in my lifetime all these sights would be lost. Perhaps it should have been a warning to us when the Beeching axe fell in the early 1960s, but we made the mistake of thinking that familiarity meant permanency and that our beloved railways were sacrosanct, which unfortunately they were not.

In those days everyone took everything

for granted, especially the staff. The free passes were never really appreciated and one tended to use them like old folk use bus passes today. We were cosseted, within the all-embracing arm of a protective employer, and we only wrenched those arms apart when we were to retire. In those far-off distant days one had to do something really appalling to get the sack, and one could be off for months without a problem from the management. It would be hard for anyone now to understand the loyalty we felt towards the railway. For the less sensitive, it must be hard to understand how we felt.

In those long-ago summers, at the weekend, it was not unusual for at least ten coaches to make up the through section of the 'Cornish Riviera' to St Ives, being pulled into the station by two '45xx' Class tanks. What a fine sight this must have been, and I can almost share the children's excitement as the line hugs the cliff to pass Carbis Bay, with its golden sand, and on into St Ives Bay. In less busy times it was more than likely that you would see the inevitable 2-6-2T prairie tank rounding the curve at Porthminster Point on its way to St Erth.

If you had been around in 1947 you could have seen an 0-6-0 pannier tank, built at the end of the 19th century, quite happily bringing a single coach into Gwinear Road. It is interesting to note that Gwinear Road had the second longest level crossing gates on the system, the longest being at Avonmouth. On a windy day the signalman would ask for the assistance of a porter to push the gates, as there was a danger of the rods breaking with the extra resistance. If that happened it would mean an urgent call to the Signal & Telegraph Department, requesting an engineer post haste to reweld the rods.

Perhaps one would have been lucky

An early view of Gwinear Road station. In the background can be seen the remarkably long level crossing gates. *Lens of Sutton*

enough to have seen a Collett 0-4-2 tank and trailer on its way between Lostwithiel and the Fowey branch, the single line following the wooded western bank of the estuary via the midway halt at Golant. This line closed for passengers in January 1965, and other lines have also long since closed, but are not forgotten, like the Fowey to St Blazey line, which lost its passenger service in 1929, although it remained open for the all-important clay traffic. It must also have been a picturesque run from Bodmin General to Bodmin Road, or along the single-track line to Boscarne Junction and on to Wadebridge, parts of which route are now thankfully preserved. And what better and more exciting experiences could there have been for a young lad, when starting work, than to see the view from Hayle viaduct and to get a glance of

Harvey's Foundry, or to slow down to pick up the tablet by the Royal Albert Bridge signal box, giving the driver permission to enter the single-track section over the Tamar into Cornwall and home.

Another adventure was the long climb up from Truro to Chacewater. I once bought in London a trilby with a feather in it, but I only owned it for a few hours. I put my head out of the window at this point, only to see my hat take flight, never to be seen again.

In Cornwall we would be transported by the ex-GWR 'Castles' and 'Halls'. Engines I remember are No 4090 *Dorchester Castle* and No 5058 *Earl of Clancarty*, the latter being one of the engines most frequently used. It was a wonderful engine with paintwork always spick and span. Another 'Castle' used on the 'Limited' was No 7031 *Cromwell's*

The Royal Albert Bridge seen from the Devon side. In the foreground is the signal box at St Budeaux where in earlier times the single line token was given to the driver to permit passage across the bridge. *W. Adams*

Days of transition: 'Castle' No 4098 *Kidwelly Castle* leads new 'Warship' Class No D602 *Bulldog*, less than two years old, hauling the 6.25am Penzance to Paddington train at Brent on 5 August 1960. Had the diesel-hydraulic locomotive failed, a not uncommon occurrence? *Hugh Ballantyne*

Castle, built in Swindon in 1950. Two others I also remember at that time were No 4095 *Harlech Castle* and 'Hall' No 4971 *Stanway Hall*, both fine engines. The 'County' Class 4-6-0s were introduced in the latter years of the GWR in 1945, and one I particularly remember was No 1002 *County of Berks*.

After Plymouth, heading north, we would be pulled by 'Kings', and what monsters these were! One day we were giving out lunch tickets on Plymouth station platform, and along came this driver. He told us it was his last day, and that he was destined to drive shunters until his retirement. He said that if given the all clear, he was going to open the engine up and we should be warned. This turned out to be the understatement of all time. That day we had *King George V* up front. I am sure I heard the brass bell, presented during the locomotive's trip to America in 1927, call out in alarm!

It was when we had a clear run up through Taunton that it was most fearful. I have no real idea what rate we were doing, but in all of my years of service I never experienced such speed. It was impossible to stand up straight. Both in the kitchen and pantry all hell was let loose. I remember seeing all three kitchen staff with their hands above their heads trying to stop all the working implements from taking flight. The water in the pantry sink was spilling over the top like some angry volcano, so much so that I had to pull out the plug. It was all we could do to stand up and hold on to the handrail. I do not wish to exaggerate, but it was one of the few times I have been truly scared. This could not go on for ever, and gradually the speed came down. None of the staff said anything. We just looked at each other, and raised our eyes to the heavens. We were into Paddington well before time.

It was not unusual for us to arrive early – it was the norm rather than the exception. We were always given priority and they would shunt anything to one side to let the 'Limited' through. One sad exception to this was when there was flooding at Exeter, and we could not get through. We were put on the Southern line and ran into Waterloo. The shame of it! To make matters worse, there was a group of Southern dining car staff hanging out of the window of their train. The gestures they made in our direction were downright obscene. We could only hang our heads. To see our beloved 'Limited' at Waterloo was like watching a beautiful woman getting into a very ugly dress!

The saddest day was when *King George V* took us into Paddington for the last time. The driver was inconsolable. The next day was not much better. We had a diesel up for the first time. I walked to the end of the platform to look at it and saw a travelling inspector and a dining car inspector standing there, with tears running down their cheeks. That day we did not leave at 10.30, as they could not get the diesel to go. How late we were I cannot now remember, but I do recollect that it was not a good omen.

Although I must admit that I find it hard to become sentimental about something made of metal, I can understand others not feeling the same as me. Perhaps it is to their credit, who knows? I do know this, that I respected and trusted those workmates, and if my destiny had been to go to war I could not have chosen a finer band of reprobates to be with, and gladly in chorus we would have shouted the Cornish anthem 'All for one and one for all'.

INDEX